Live Bait
Tactics

Live Bait Tactics

Complete Angler's Library ®
North American Fishing Club
Minneapolis, Minnesota

Live Bait Tactics

Copyright © 1993, North American Fishing Club

Library of Congress Catalog Card Number 93-83706
ISBN 0-914697-55-2

Printed in U.S.A.
4   5   6   7   8   9

Contents

Acknowledgments

The North American Fishing Club would like to thank all those who helped create this book.

Wildlife artist Virgil Beck created the cover art. Artist David Rottinghaus provided all inside illustrations, except for prepared line drawings from Berkley and Mustad. Photos, in addition to the author's, were provided by Chris Altman, Annette Bignami, Soc Clay, Paul DeMarchi, Bill Hilts Jr., Dave Hrbacek, North American Fisherman Editor Steve Pennaz, C. Boyd Pfeiffer and Dale Spartas.

A special thanks to the NAFC's publication staff for all their efforts, including Publisher Mark LaBarbera, North American Fisherman Editor Steve Pennaz, Managing Editor of Books Ron Larsen, Associate Editor of Books Colleen Ferguson and Editorial Assistant of Books Victoria Brouillette. Thanks also go to Vice President of Product Marketing Mike Vail, Marketing Manager Cal Franklin and Marketing Project Coordinator Laura Resnik.

About The Author

L ouis Bignami claims that he has never used a bait he didn't like, and he's used some strange ones. He admits that he began considering nearly everything as potential bait when his mother began packing sardine sandwiches in his school lunch pail. Meadow mice also caught his eye for their bait potential, as did a number of critters which can be best described as "exotics." On the flip side, he has found himself casting a gourmet's eye upon other baits such as good looking shrimp or crayfish, and the thought of "wasting" such tasty tidbits on mere fish created a real dilemma. Lou who has, along with his wife, Annette, authored cookbooks shelved his thoughts about eating long enough to write this comprehensive volume on the use of live bait.

Live Bait Tactics is Lou's second complete book for the Complete Angler's Library series, the other being Stories Behind Record Fish. He also has contributed to several North American Fishing Club cookbooks.

In nearly 50 years of fishing, Lou has seen the resurgence of bait fishing in this country, despite rumors of its demise. During the years he fished San Francisco Bay, live herring became the favored bait for sturgeon. He was among the early users of crayfish tails for steelhead in California waters, as well as pushing the use of leeches on lower-elevation California trout streams. His uncles, who had fished for stripers in the days when goldfish were a

favored and legal bait and five-fish limits topped out at 100 pounds or more, showed him how to freeline shiners for stripers and anchovy for salmon. He has studied live-bait methods in Hawaii, Central America and much of Europe, as well as the highly unique methods used by Upper Midwest ice anglers to protect bait from the bone-chilling cold.

Lou who resides in Idaho turned to writing about the outdoors after pursuing possible careers in field archaeology, banking, professional tennis, the U.S. Army and in real estate management. Having graduated from college and law school, as well as working as a bank trust officer, Lou began writing. He has sold several thousand articles and photographs, and has authored or co-authored with his wife nearly a dozen books.

A member of the Outdoor Writers Association of America, Lou has won several OWAA awards for his writing, and is a member of the Society of Professional Journalists and the American Society of Journalists and Authors.

Dedication

Nobody fishes alone. We tote the memories of trips present and past. In time, results improve and stories read may become stories lived. Eventually it becomes difficult to credit those who led us gently to our favorite avocation.

When "real fishermen" fished only for salmon, trout, striped bass and steelhead, Dad headed out through the Golden Gate for salmon, and spent summers backpacking to trout streams. Mom took us kids to the pier and was sufficiently "piscatorially compulsive" to fish for striped bass even on Thanksgiving Day.

My first exposure to bait came from "Johnny," the man with the long cane pole and small green box with shoulder strap who showed me how he caught at least 10 times as many jack smelt with pile worms as anyone else. Even then, light gear, small hooks and practice paid dividends.

This book is dedicated to those whose articles and books showed the way, especially to Frank Woolner whose loving editing helped so many early writers survive, to "Uncle" Homer Circle who deserves special credit for his six decades of sensible prose and to Ed Park who helped hone my early prose.

Foreword

Without a doubt, one of the most often asked questions in fishing is: What did you catch it on?

For the angler, it is an important fact-finding question. For if we can determine what interests the gamefish we are pursuing, then we can quickly get about the business of catching fish. It's also at the bottom of the sometimes intense debates about which is the more effective fish-catcher—live bait or skillfully engineered artificials?

Skillful anglers have long recognized that there are very specific advantages to both live bait and artificials. Both have their days, but when fishing is really tough many anglers switch to live bait. After all, no matter how carefully an artificial lure is manufactured, it can't begin to duplicate a living, moving organism. And because we want to help you catch more fish, even on the toughest days on the water, we felt that a book about fishing with live bait was in order.

Live bait certainly is not a new subject. It is as old as fishing itself. But the idea of using live objects found within the piscatorial food chain—and even outside of it—as bait has lost ground to the technological explosion of lures that are highly successful imitations of the real thing. *Live Bait Tactics* tells the story of the advantages of fishing with live bait and provides tips for rigging and fishing that will help you catch more fish.

In this volume, our author—Lou Bignami—has unearthed information about many different baits. You may be familiar with some but even if you're a veteran live-bait angler, you probably haven't used all the baits—or rigs—covered here. After all, as Lou notes in the book, there are more than 1,000 different types of live bait. If you start multiplying that figure by the number of different combinations, you're talking thousands of options. Of course, many of you have specialized in fishing for certain species of gamefish, but you may discover from reading this volume that there are more baits and more combinations that will work than you may have realized.

The point here is that bait fishing can be as complex a pursuit as NAFC members want to make it. With the attention given to fishing with artificials, it's easy to forget that most anglers take fish with live bait. In fact, day in and day out, there is nothing more effective than putting a gamefish's natural forage in front of its nose.

But it's not just a matter of simply stabbing a minnow or a worm with a hook and tossing it into the water. Gamefish can be fickle predators whose diets change as different forages become available and then disappear. These fish generally are very opportunistic feeders, looking for "easy" meals so they don't burn up more energy going after prey than they obtain by catching it. So there also are tips offered in this book on how to present the bait more naturally while keeping in mind that a struggling, or possibly injured, minnow is going to be more attractive to a hungry, but energy-conscious predator. It also re-enforces the "match the hatch" theory of bait selection.

You'll find in here a discussion of live bait by type. Types include minnows, other baitfish such as alewives and shad, worms of all kinds, leeches, various amphibians such as frogs, toads and salamanders, crustaceans including crayfish, shrimp, mussels and clams, aquatic and terrestrial insects and their larvae and nymphs. You also will learn about which gamefish seem most attracted to which baits, including the widespread appeal of worms even though most worms used as bait in freshwater are not aquatic.

The author also emphasizes proper care of live bait so that it will remain robust before and while you're fishing, as lively bait generally catches more fish—but there are exceptions to that rule, too. Sometimes, larger fish are more attracted to live bait that appears to be injured; the author tells you how to create that look.

Tips also are offered on how to tell whether the minnows you are buying at the bait shop are in good condition; what to do if the bait shop doesn't carry the type of bait that you want; and how to collect and grow your own bait.

Fishing should be, above all else, fun! *Live Bait Tactics* will unlock some of the secrets of why fish respond the way they do to different presentations at various times of the season; why some baits are dynamite in the spring and early summer, but duds in late summer and fall. With this knowledge you will be a more effective angler, and your enjoyment of the sport will increase.

That's why we know you will want to read *Live Bait Tactics*. Good fishing!

Steve Pennaz
Executive Director
North American Fishing Club

The Mechanics
Of Bait Fishing

1

Bait Fishing Through The Ages

Bait works best! At most times and in most places, live bait will take more fish than artificials. The advantages of live bait increases as conditions get tough, fishing pressures increase or the angler makes a conscious effort to concentrate on taking trophy fish.

Clearly, a properly selected, fresh, live bait presented on appropriate tackle in a subtle manner suits today's conditions for the beginner and expert alike. For example, nothing beats a big, live shiner for bass in the summer heat when fishing is slow. No nymph pattern works better than a live hellgrammite drifted to a picky brown trout on a rocky mountain stream. If live baits did not work so well they would not be banned in so many places, right?

The reason live bait works best is simple. Even though incredible amounts of ingenuity and tons of technology are brought to focus on artificial lure shape, color, action and, yes, taste, fish still know the difference. That's not just piscatorial. Is any imitation ever better than the real thing? Margarine may look like butter, but a gourmet knows the difference. Gourmet fish, the survivors of today's piscatorial wars, know the difference, too.

Bait-Fishing History

Early man used crudely fashioned fish hooks baited with who knows what to take fish. Unfortunately, not much in the way of primitive fishing tackle survives. The earliest tackle seems to be some Stone-Age hooks from eastern Europe. Clearly, early man

Tony Dempsey claimed a world-record warmouth (2 pounds, 7 ounces) in Florida in 1985. He joined the list of anglers who have caught a record fish with live bait—in this case, a wiggler.

Bait Fishing Through The Ages

fished with bait. Hair lines and wood poles obviously wouldn't survive, but language does. In Latin and in Hebrew the same word means both "thorn" and "hook," providing us with a glimpse into the past.

Fishing hasn't always had a good image. Plato called it "a lazy deceitful occupation, unworthy of a gentleman;" however, the Romans thought that fishing was a suitable occupation because it "encourages contemplation." The first authenticated literary mention of fishing was by an Aeolian who used natural flies to catch fish. He talked about converting pesky mosquitoes into bait. Perhaps he used craneflies or maybe he just told a fish story. Aeolians also started the glut of fishing literature on artificial flies.

Why do so many fishermen look down on bait even though most experts agree that bait fishing is, at its most sophisticated, both the most productive and the most subtle form of the sport? Why do many claim some higher art exists with lures and flies? After all, Dame Juliana Berners published her *Bok of St. Albans* or *Treatise of Fishing with an Angle* in 1496, and she meant angle worms, not ways to skirt fish and game regulations!

Shortly after Dame Berners, the Middle Ages produced Izaak Walton's *The Complete Angler*.

A cynic might note that one reason bait fishing gets little ink these days is that bait sellers don't advertise much; however, most bait fishermen—except for the walleye subset—don't get very enthused about fishing tournaments and all their accoutrements either. The separation in status of live bait and artificials predates fishing tournaments as we know them today.

The same Industrial Revolution that helped the rich afford to fish for trout with flies helped the common man fish—even though that wasn't the intention. Affordable hooks became commercially available from firms like Partridge—you no longer had to create your own hooks out of bent needles.

Rail transport improved and, indirectly supported by freight fees, average anglers could now reach and fish canals cut for commercial transportation. This created waterway highways, enabling fish to move from one major body of water to another.

Such canals held unwanted fish, such as trench, carp and zander (European walleye), as well as a host of tiddlers like our bluegills. British workingmen still use "simple" magnum-length cane poles to catch such fish. Immigrants brought these skills and

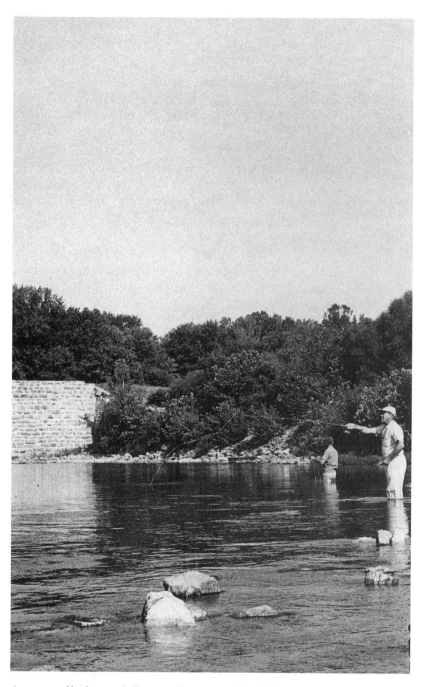

Areas created by dams on shallow rivers have proven to be productive places to fish with live bait for smallmouths and panfish.

inclinations to America to be carried on by each generation.

These simple poles remain an effective fishing tool today. Don't believe it? A Frenchman used this kind of rig to take over 600 fish on a single hook—in one hour. Admittedly, these were small fish. However, it's been repeatedly demonstrated that a pole expert who rigs with stump grubs or hellgrammites and is equipped to wade can take more trout per hour in pocket water than a fly fisherman.

It's also worth noting that the poles used by European "match" anglers, the proper British equivalent of our bass pros, look simple; however, the latest state-of-the-art graphite wonders ranging up to 40 feet in length can cost as much as $4,000!

When European fishing traditions moved to America, some of the same distinctions pertained. "Gentlemen" caught trout with flies—really artificial insects. "Others" took striped bass from the surf and other fish from inland waters with live bait. In most cases, the angler collected the bait himself.

Early American fishermen definitely ranked as piscatorial elitists. In most areas, only salmon, trout, steelhead and, perhaps, striped bass counted. Other species such as black bass, particularly smallmouths, were classed as "rough" fish, sharing the lowly status of carp.

Like most wars, World War II resulted in a major change in American fishing. Manpower movements brought East Coast bluefish buffs to Pacific Northwest steelhead streams and Sierra trout, but bait fishing remained the most popular method. However, war technology, as always, spawned major improvements in fishing-tackle technology. Monofilament lines, spinning reels, development of fiberglass and even more advanced rod materials and injection moldings along with a host of other improvements changed the image of fishing. No more soaking leaders or drying linen lines overnight, and no more bamboo rod fractures!

The post-war years saw the start of freeway networks making it possible for fishermen to reach once inaccessible waters for a weekend outing. At this point, bass fishing spilled out of the smallmouth waters of the Northeast, and largemouth waters in the Southwest grew behind new dams being built for energy purposes. Salmon, trout, steelhead and smallmouth streams drowned by hydropower's needs became "structure" for bass addicts. With so many relatively unschooled fish available, fishing with artific-

The development of hydropower around the country also created new opportunities for bait anglers. These anglers are using minnows and other bait to entice tailrace catfish.

ials grew in popularity. Fishermen, flushed with post-war dollars, had both the hours and the money to spend on their sport. Higher tech meant higher price tags and more emphasis on the "technology" of fishing. As a result, today's bass boat and gear costs more than a middle class home did in 1946.

However, today's conditions, both economic and otherwise, suggest that bait fishing is on its way back to being the most affordable, effective method.

Facing greater competition for income dollars, anglers are finding big-ticket fishing items harder to justify. Fortunately, fishing still lets adults and kids share "quality time"—even if on a more limited basis.

To get the most action out of today's precious leisure time, only the most productive method—live bait—makes sense. Bait

Bait Fishing Through The Ages

gear costs a lot less, too! Why invest so much time, energy and money in lures and flies when most of the fish caught in North America still bite bait. This will, in the long term, help fishing survive as a bucolic pleasure.

Close-To-Home Action

Live bait—where it's not prohibited—can take a variety of gamefish right around home. You should invest in a 5-foot ultra-light rig and some terminal tackle and let neighborhood panfish challenge your skills. For children, rig a simple cane pole with a bobber, small hook and a lively worm—you've eliminated a lot of tackle hassle. Fishing with live bait can be simple and inexpensive because terminal tackle costs are small. You can save even more if you make your own bobbers, cast your own weights and wrap your own rods. Bait fishing is great sport; it can be one of the most complex forms of fishing in freshwater!

Over 1,000 different live baits are possible if you add up the many species of minnows, baitfish, worms, leeches, frogs, toads, salamanders, crayfish, shrimp, aquatic insects, terrestrial insects and larvae that will be covered in this volume. Compound this with double rigs—where legal—that let you offer two or more baits at a time. Consider the multitude of hook choices to match the variety of live bait sizes and types, the addition of dead or preserved baits and the host of bobbers designed for different techniques in still and moving waters.

Compound the many bobbers, sinkers and lure/bait combinations possible and it's clear that mastery of live-bait fishing in all of its complexity is as likely as winning a lottery. Fortunately, one need not master everything about bait fishing to catch fish the first time out. It's comforting, however, to know that the challenge exists.

Catch-And-Release Bait Fishing

In many jurisdictions, fish-and-game organizations prohibit the use of live bait to limit the harvesting of fish. They usually, however, reduce catch limits first. Live bait is banned on the theory that bait fishing results in more dead fish than does fishing with lures or flies. Obviously, this does not need to be the case. Skilled bait anglers with sophisticated gear can set barbless or conventional hooks quickly, preventing the swallowing of hooks.

Bait hooks do not need to be any larger than hooks used on artificials. Barbless bait hooks work well, too.

Some fish will swallow the hook; however, it does not need to be fatal. Clip the leader, leaving the hook in place to rust away. Extensive research supports that decent survival rates are realized when a hook is left in place.

History proves that bait fishing is the most effective way to take fish. For most anglers, as expertise and access grow and larger catches become possible, only the parallel appreciation of the opportunity, the joy of fishing and the desire to allow those who come after to share the sport, limit the take.

Plain And Fancy Fishing

Children have the right idea about fishing. They look for action and don't mind dangling a worm. Until influenced by adults, they maintain a desire to catch small fish with simple tackle close to home with minimum time spent in transit. This is accompanied by maximum effort in watching bugs, checking the scenery or skipping stones. Adults who don't have to prove anything to anyone on or at the water can share this happy approach and help maintain healthy fisheries.

2

Realistic Rods And Reels, Lusty Lines

L ively baits produce results that even make the inexpensive rod, reel and line packages work better than expected. However, as George Orwell reminds us, "Some are more equal than others." The right rod, reel and line combined with the proper bait and terminal tackle for the conditions and type of fish you are seeking radically improve results. The choice of a rod, it must be noted, is more important than the reel selection for bait fishing. The reason for this is two-fold. First, the reel's basic function is to hold line. Second, rods help the angler "sense" a bite and set the hook, as well as relay the bait's reactions to its environment.

The requirements for bait fishing are somewhat different than those for artificial lure or fly fishing. For example, you must keep bait on the hook. A soft rodtip and gentle sidearm cast are needed, and mending line on the drift is also required. Similar to fly fishing, a longer rod and cast help place the bait in the most productive area. If all else is equal, you can cast farther with a longer rod. Unfortunately, American bait fishermen enamored with the lengthy "noodle" rods only have part of the game right. Noodle rods are helpful in playing big fish on light tackle; however, casting is a problem. They simply do not present a bait as accurately as does the British-style rod with its stiffer butt and more flexible tip.

Specifically designed long rods are used for trolling live bait; they increase the effective spread of bait presentation while withstanding the added stress from the trolling action.

There are rods for nearly every purpose in bait fishing. Selecting from the numerous rods available can be confusing for even the most serious anglers.

The Terminal Test

In selecting the right rod, the first thing to check is the weight it tosses best, and how that relates to the total weight of the terminal tackle you'll be using. Other things being equal, lighter is better. Look for the lightest rod that will cover your needs. For example, if you fish unweighted worms in moving water, a small ultra-light rod rated for ⅛- to ½-ounce terminal tackle and bait could be the best choice. If you will be casting massive suckers for pike, a rod rated for 2, 3 or more ounces will work best.

Although these ratings relate to line test, there is a proportional relationship between terminal tackle weight and line test which varies from rod to rod. These ratings can be useful in matching your needs.

Rod Selection: Length, Action And Quality

Rod length depends more on your presentation and the water in which you're fishing than the species you are seeking. Typically, American rods and poles are shorter than those used in Europe. Long rods and poles are a major advantage for bank anglers; however, those who fish from boats will have more difficulty. Long rods don't suit brush, unless telescopic. Longer rods, especially the less expensive ones, feel "heavy" when the balance point (that special feel) is too far forward. You can, to a certain extent, correct this "imbalance" by using a larger reel or weighting the butt with lead. European bait rods all feature longer, heavier butts. More and more American rods are featuring longer butts every year. Clearly, two-handed butts offer better control and relieve pressure which causes shoulder and arm injuries, such as "caster's elbow."

Longer and stiffer rods generally offer more distance and control with most baits, and a fast tip offers the maximum casting leverage. However, it requires skill not to cast off bait. Noodle sticks cast easily with bait for just about anyone.

Rod materials don't affect the action nearly as much as the rod designer's skill and the manufacturer's reputation. The most expensive materials, such as the top-line graphites, offer more stiffness for the weight. These materials, worked into very small diameter rods with less wind resistance on the longer models, balance better without excessively heavy butt sections.

As a rule, lighter weight and more sophisticated designs come

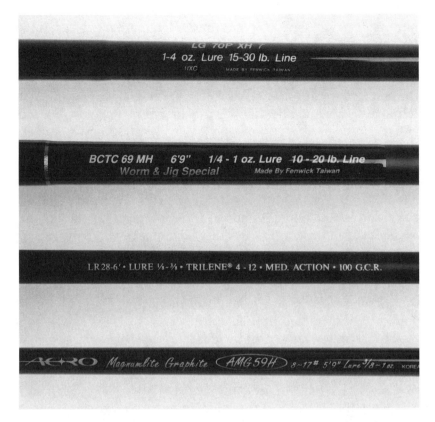

When choosing a rod, make sure to read the information from the manufacturer that is stamped on the rod blank. It tells you what weight bait and terminal tackle the rod is designed to handle.

at the price of decreased durability in any kind of gear. Those who hold rods all day and cast often, such as fly fishermen, will want to pay the premium required for added durability. Anglers who bounce baits along river- or streambeds where it's helpful to "feel" the bottom will find it advantageous to pay the higher price.

Overall, graphite seems the material of choice for bait-fishing rods used to bounce baits on the bottom. This is because graphite successfully transmits the vibrations of even the lightest bites. Less expensive fiberglass works if bobbers are used because you usually see bites before you feel them. Fiberglass is a decent choice for sedentary lake fishing where rod weight isn't a serious burden.

Appropriate rods for bait fishing range downward in size from the monster 12- to 15-foot surf-casting rigs, which can plunk an alewife past a Great Lakes shore break in a howling gale, to 5-foot ultra-light rigs designed to pitch tiny hellgrammites at brook trout lurking in a brushy, rushing stream pocket.

Judging rod quality in the store isn't too difficult. Usually, rods in the middle of a name-brand manufacturer's price range offer the best long-term values. If you're on a tight budget, buy the best terminal tackle and line that you can afford and upgrade your rod and reel later. Seeking a multi-purpose rod is another way of staying within a limited budget. An 8- to 9-foot-long, medium action "steelhead" rod in graphite with a two-handed grip may be the closest thing to an all-around bait-fishing rod on the market. Such a rod offers a reasonably soft action, allowing the bait to stay on better. A decent quality 9-footer makes line mending in moving water easier and offers some leverage advantages in moving fish up and over obstacles. You obtain extra casting distance from bank or boat and, when trolling two such rods, better separation between baits. Such "two-handed" rods reduce casting fatigue, as well as the strain on arms, shoulders and elbows—an important point for those with joint problems.

Fly fishermen know that fly rods offer superb presentations of floating baits or bottom-bouncing baits with fly lines if false casts are limited.

Bait anglers who fish from the shores of lakes or big river banks where casting distance is critical might want to switch to 10- or even 12-foot, moderately light action rods that maximize casting distance and help control the bait at a distance. In England, where bait or "course" fishing is the norm, "float" rods aimed at those who fish with bobbers run to 15 feet in length, connecting in three pieces. "Ledger" rods, designed for bottom fishing, run from 9 to 11 feet in length and feature special tips which detect even the lightest bites. Such rods offer major advantages for bank fishermen in most situations. If you opt for a longer rod, however, consider buying a long-handled net. Even a professional basketball player's arms aren't long enough to easily land a large fish with a 12-foot rod and a 2-foot net!

Extra long rods do not perform well on thickly overgrown streams; therefore, small-stream specialists find a shorter, 4- to 6-foot ultra-light rod handy around thick cover. Shorter rods offer solid action when fishing for panfish and trout from boat or bank where casting distance isn't critical and 2- to 4-pound-test line is appropriate. These rods also work well for urban anglers who use

Live shiners can be fished successfully on all these rigs. Fly-rod outfits aren't just for use with artificials anymore. Smaller live baits work, too.

public transportation or want a greater challenge with panfish. Combining them with a long rod for lakes, you can cover most piscatorial possibilities.

With heavy baits, cover or fish, heavy-duty bait-casting rods armed with 20- to 25-pound-test line get the nod. Hefty fish, like muskies or pike, and tough conditions, such as entangling lily pads or thick nasty cover, require tougher gear that works well with big baits, like large minnows and suckers. Bait-casting rigs work best with 20-pound-test line (or more) and heavy bait. Consider rods with the longer-than-average tips and the longer straight grips that allow the angler to make two-handed hauls from the thick stuff. In extremely heavy cover, some, like the California fishermen who developed "flippin" with their striped bass rods from the beach, find that even surf tackle is appropriate.

Realistic Rods And Reels, Lusty Lines

Roll Your Own

It's easy to make good long rods from fly-rod blanks. Opt for a long, cork grip sized to fit your hands. The butt should be long enough so you can cast with two hands and fit it under your arm while you reel. If you fish in cold weather, forget about metal reel seats and simply tape the reel in place. You can also inexpensively make light, short rods to use on streams or for ice fishing.

Use of extremely light guides, such as single-foot Fujis or Foulproof, will maintain the rod balance at just under the reel. Add a crutch tip to the rod butt for additional weight and, if it's still too light, insert some lead inside the butt.

Finding Pleasure With A Pole

In extremely thick cover, you can't beat a pole that, unlike a rod, doesn't require a reel. Nothing takes more fish faster. In Europe, as mentioned in Chapter 1, the record for fish caught on a single rig in an hour is 600! While cane poles suit traditionalists, nesting fiberglass or, if you can find one, graphite poles in the 16- to 20-foot range offer major advantages for panfishing. Really long poles provide quiet presentations, a direct drop to fish even in the heaviest cover and a chance to bring in fish by skipping them over weeds and other hazards.

A nesting fiberglass pole offers a decent start for those new to the simple looking but very sophisticated method. Even though these poles are ideal for introducing kids to fishing, they are definitely not a "kid's toy." No other tool offers such a delicate presentation of light insects on trout waters or the chance to lower succulent baits to hefty bass in the deepest cover.

The Reel Stuff

Your choice of reel will vary with the conditions. Fly, spincast, spinning, baitcasting or European pin-type and rotating reels all have their place. You probably already own a suitable reel. Medium-priced, medium-quality models offer maximum value for most bait fishermen who, with the exception of a few dedicated stream anglers, cast and reel less often than artificial lure chuckers. Generally, spinning reels spooled with lines of less than 15-pound test best combine ease of operation with greater casting distance for those with average casting skills.

For higher line-test casting and trolling, levelwind baitcasting

A wide array of reels is available to the sport fisherman, also. The basic types include spinning, spincasting, baitcasting and fly reels. Each type has its purpose.

reels suit most needs. Revolving-spool reels were, after all, once called "bait casters," and this is not accidental! With skilled handling of these reels, baits can be more accurately presented with less line-jerking than with spinning reels. If you get excited, however, you may lose this advantage. When using spinning reels, most anglers find drag control with the thumb more convenient than with the fingertip.

Spincasting reels work well within their limitations of restricted casting range and limited line capacity. Some ultra-light experts do well with these reels, and the close-faced reels aren't a bad choice for brook fishing, either. They are, after all, relatively easy to use for most fishing situations.

Fly reels suit tiny live-bait presentations requiring fly lines. More specialized reels, such as trolling models with sophisticated drags and the Alvey, a flip-flop, butt-mounted Australian reel designed for maximum distance casting, deserve a look, too. British anglers use "centre-pin reels" which are similar to large fly reels on fast, strong-running rivers. These reels are showing up in U.S. tackle boxes, especially in the king salmon enclaves of the Pacific Northwest.

The Quality Question

For the average angler who fishes less than 30 days a year, medium-priced, mid-line reels are a bargain. With top-of-the-line reels priced well over $100, it's clear that many anglers pay for performance and features that they do not need. Pros and guides who fish 200 or more days a year need more durable equipment. Today, most fishermen can get great performance from reels in the $15 to $30 range. These reels can serve you well for a decade or more if they are lubricated every season. Saltwater reels should be rinsed in freshwater after every use. Wise fishermen also release the reel's drag after every trip. This ensures maximum smoothness without the "buzz, pause, buzz" that signals a deformed drag washer and a sticking drag.

Open-Faced Spinning Reels

If properly loaded with quality line to within ⅛ inch of the spool rim, open-faced spinning reels will provide maximum casting distance at line weights bait anglers normally use. A major feature is their interchangeable spool capability. Available in both short and large capacity models, extra spools with different line choices enable you to fine-tune presentations quickly.

Larger diameter spool reels coupled with rods with larger guides give you the greatest casting distance and retrieval speed. When selecting a reel, you should be sure that its centerline aims at the first, or gathering, guide on your rod. This minimizes line friction during the cast, maximizing the distance. Night-fishermen might want to obtain old manual pickup models. These eliminate incomplete bail closures and can be operated by "feel" in the dark.

Open-faced reel drags vary in location and quality. Rear drag systems are easier to adjust during a fight—assuming you remember to turn the knob the right way—but are easily bumped. Front drags are better protected; however, on some models, the cost is catching line under the adjustment knob.

Spinning and spincasting reels shouldn't be used for trolling; the line will kink if you reel against the drag.

Casting Considered

Unfortunately, a soft bait tends to remove itself from the hook when an angler using a spinning reel holds the line in the crease of

'Feathering' A Cast With Fragile Bait

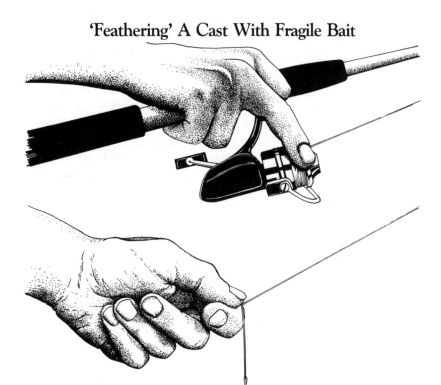

Controlling the line flow with your finger enables you to cast fragile bait without it turning into chum. Featuring the cast with your finger takes practice, however.

the forefinger during a cast. A soft bait should be presented with a gentle sidearm cast while pinning the line against the reel spool with the tip of your forefinger. It is quite easy, then, to simply lift your fingertip off the line, allowing the bait to leave without a jerk. It's easy—and advised—to gently feather line spinning off the reel. This controls the length of your cast and ensures minimal slack when the bait hits the water. If there is an immediate hit, simply jam your forefinger against the spool, set the hook, close the bail and reel.

When you have a fish at net or are heading for a snag, you can also use your forefinger to radically increase drag on the reel spool. By doing this, you eliminate the 80-percent chance of turning the drag the wrong way when fighting the fish. This mistake usually will result in a broken line and a lost fish.

Close-Faced Reels

Quality models offer decent value and advantages in very heavy cover with less snagging. However, range is reduced and the chance of major tangles under the hood is increased. They do work nicely, however, with fly rods as auxiliary reels—check the Fre-Line model that spins line off the center of the spool. Models that hang under the reel, rather than perch on top, seem to balance best. Top-mounted reels suit boaters because their position keeps line on top of the rod to reduce snagging on gunwales during the action.

Baitcasting Reels

Aside from their well-known propensity for building birds' nests on the spool at the most inconvenient times, baitcasting reels offer major advantages, especially when trolling live baits or cranking against the drag. Skilled fishermen find that an educated thumb and a gentle sidearm cast are the keys to smoothly accelerating the bait. This allows soft baits to stay on, and the infamous backlash is averted. In many cases, baitcasting gear can be more accurate than spinning tackle, too. However, some reels will hang light line tests behind the spool. Overall, such reels seem ideally suited for larger species such as steelhead, pike or muskies.

Fly Reels

Simple single-action or multiplying fly reels handle fly lines as advertised and can, in a pinch, work for trolling. Their major problem, aside from casting distance, is a slow retrieval speed. Models with exposed spools that let you add extra drag when needed seem to be the best choice. Spring-driven fly reels, like the popular Martin reels, can retrieve a lot of line quickly. If you can keep them from freezing, they work nicely with extra rigs on the ice.

Specialized Reels

The European centre-pin reel functions much like a large-diameter fly reel. It works well for downstream drift fishing and when used in specialized floating techniques. Large-diameter revolving spool reels are the best choice for wire or lead-core-line trolling and bottomfishing in deep waters. Serious trollers also might consider expensive 20- or 30-pound line-class offshore reels

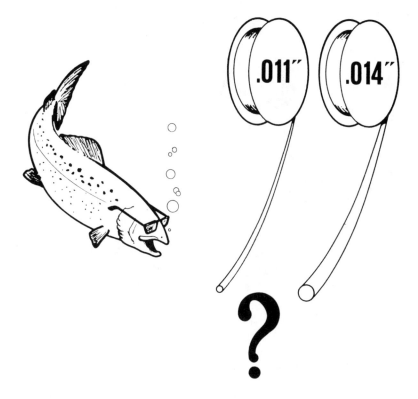

Selecting fishing line based upon diameter can pay big dividends when you're after easily spooked gamefish. A smaller-diameter line can mean the difference between getting a full limit or being skunked.

used by light-tackle deep-sea fishermen. Other unusual options include the half-turn rotation of the Alvey reel that offers astonishing casting distances when mounted at the butt of a 15-foot surf rod outfitted with oversized guides. However, line twists occur at the most inconvenient times.

Understanding Line Test Ratings

Most fishermen buy line by test rather than by diameter. So line manufacturers tend to offer "the strongest 10-pound-test line on the market," which, in reality, may test 14 pounds! In a recent set of tests, for example, 10-pound-test lines broke anywhere from 10.2 to 18.8 pounds. Even methods to test line vary. Some manufacturers test line dry; some test it wet. Thus, line choice based on labels is confusing. Line choice becomes simple if you're select-

Bait anglers also have a wide selection of fishing lines. Obviously a line must match the conditions, the size of your quarry and, of course, the tackle you're using.

ing lines based on diameter rather than test poundage.

Using lighter-than-average line almost always improves results. In clear-water tests with lures—the results of which also should apply to live bait—trout hit twice as often on 2-pound test as on 4-pound test; they didn't hit at all on 8-pound test. Therefore, where snags are not a problem and you're fishing off bottom, a line with a test weight equal to the weight of the largest fish you usually catch will work. Double this if you fish bottom or in cover; 6-pound bass on 12-pound test still seems to be sporting. Changing line test when you change baits improves presentations, but an extra spool is required. Two extra spools will let you cover the bases. Buying line in bulk, ¼-pound spools, is a good idea because it costs less per foot. You should also tote an extra 100-yard spool of line in case you get spooled by a big fish or suffer a bad case of the terminal kinks!

Line Materials And Choices

Monofilament, cofilament and other transparent lines come in large selections. Choices seem to change every month. If you buy line in bulk or on reel-filling spools and change lines every 10 trips, you should do well with almost any manufactured brand. Deals and discounts do seem common and are worth the search.

Complete Angler's Library

With lines under 6-pound test, choose greater flexibility over abrasion-resistance. Between 6- and 15-pound tests, regular lines for general fishing work well. However, if you fish baits where snags are prevalent, opt for lines with greater abrasion-resistance.

All monofilament lines can be damaged by ultraviolet radiation and extreme heat, so don't store your gear in hot places or in the sun. Also, take the time to fill each reel spool to the recommended level. If you overfill, you'll be casting off loops or jamming levelwinds. If you don't fill it enough, you will reduce casting distance.

3

Hooks, Sinkers And Floats

E very bait angler should have the words, "Put your money where the fish's mouth is," engraved on the top of his or her tackle box. Hooks come in more shapes, sizes and styles, and get less attention, than any other part of the bait angler's tackle. Why some anglers pay big bucks for quality rods, reels and premium line and then use cheap snelled hooks remains as much a puzzle as anglers who don't know how to tie improved clinch or Trilene knots! Sinkers and floats, the other legs of your presentation tripod, also deserve more attention than most fishermen devote to them. No other tackle item offers such potential for success at such a small price!

Proper Hook Selection Important

Hook selection may be the most critical decision you face. Even inappropriate baits will catch something if a sharp hook of the proper size and type is used. Proper selection starts with knowing the parts of a hook. It continues with selecting hooks from solid sources such as Mustad, Tru-Turn, Eagle Claw, Partridge and Gamakatsu. Avoid those 25-cents-a-package bargain wonders; if the knots don't break, the barbs will!

Each component of a hook offers a specific contribution to the hook's overall effectiveness, so pay close attention to your options.

Parts Of A Hook

Hook eyes come either down, up or in-line. Down means the

Complete Angler's Library

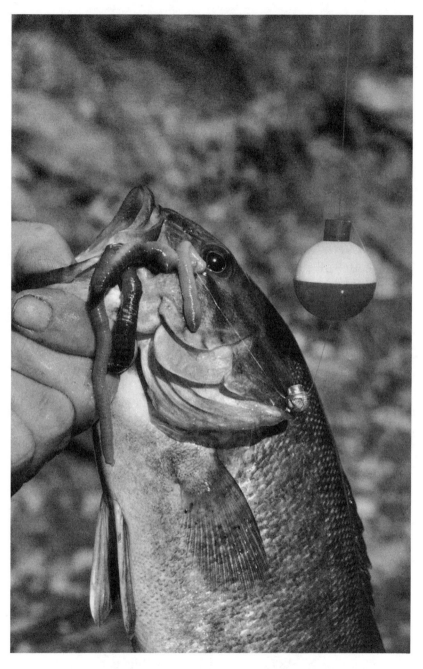

While anglers will invest a lot of money in rods and reels, they often overlook the business end of the rig—the hook, sinkers and float. These items can mean the difference between catching fish and not catching fish.

Hooks, Sinkers And Floats

eye is canted inward toward the point; up means canted out away from the point. Most bait hooks come with eyes turned down because the hook point will supposedly be pulled into the fish. However, turning the eye down decreases the effective distance between the eye and hook point. (This can be a limiting factor with short-shanked hooks.) It's the reason eyes on salmon-egg hooks are turned up. Hooks with canted eyes, whether turned up or down, are easy to snell. Hooks with in-line eyes are a good overall choice for those who use conventional knots, rather than snelling the hook. (Some manufacturers sell "big eye" hooks that even far-sighted anglers can attach.) Open-eyed hooks that can be squeezed shut on wire leaders or spinner shank eyes can reduce the frustration factor, too.

Hook shanks range from the extra-long streamer fly or bait-hook models like the Carlisle to ultra-short egg hooks that seem all bent. These are designated as 2X, 3X or 6X, meaning the shank length is multiplied by the number. Some nymph hooks come in intermediate shank lengths and curved shapes for fly-tiers. These are highly recommended for use with naturals, too. As with gaps, shanks should suit bait sizes.

Some shanks are curved to line up with the point, such as hooks primarily designed for plastic worms. These work well for trolling, too. Some hook shanks, like Tru-Turns, are twisted to ensure a better hookset. These work well if they don't cause your bait to roll, twisting the line.

As a general rule, long baits, such as worms, do best on long hooks. (A worm threaded on a long hook is less likely to curl up into the typical worm ball in the hook throat.) Long shanks also protect monofilament leaders and lines from toothy fish, such as pike. If you're using tough marine worms that slide up the shank of a long hook when a fish bites, you can easily slide them back down and use them again. Eleven jack smelt on a single, durable pile worm may be the record.

Hook-gap numbers tend to confuse anglers because the critical distance is often between the hook eye and point—not the point and shank. However, these numbers offer a way to compare different sizes: with small hooks, the larger the number the smaller the size; for big hooks (starting at 1/0), the bigger the number the bigger the hook. Differences among various manufacturers' "same-sized" hooks remain despite periodic attempts within the industry

Complete Angler's Library

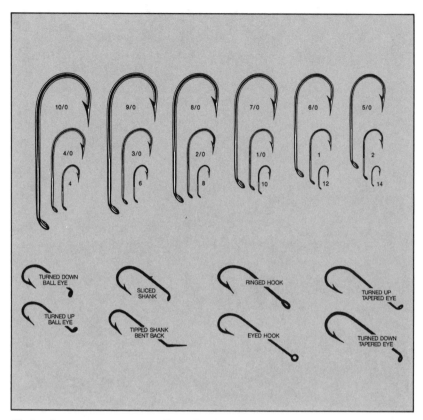

Hooks of various patterns are usually produced in a typical range of sizes as indicated in this illustration (top). Hooks come in various configurations (bottom).

to standardize hooks to eliminate the confusion.

It's important to have a selection of hooks in different sizes. You should have hooks that are a size larger, as well as smaller, than the average size needed for a given bait. This enables you to change hooks when bait sizes change. Buy loose hooks—even if you use snelled hooks. Why buy quality line in the exact test needed, and then use whatever snell weight the manufacturer happens to provide? Tying your own snells or leaders with line about 20 to 25 percent lighter than your main line will minimize the amount of terminal tackle the river goblins ingest.

The Point Is The Difference

Hook points make the difference in hook performance. Shorter points set easier; longer points with long barbs, such as

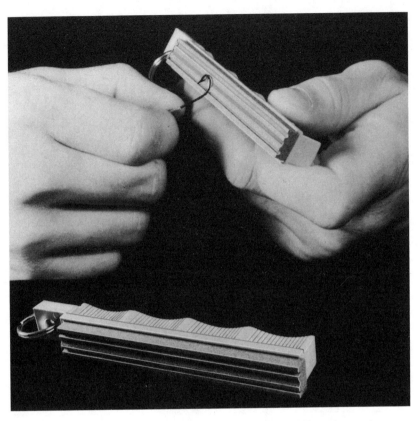

Hook sharpeners come in different shapes and sizes. This sharpener is the perfect size for storing in a tackle box or pocket. Keep sharpeners handy to touch up your hook points.

the salmon fisherman's Siwash, hold better. Hollow points and various acid- and laser-sharpened points also set more easily than spear points that are more durable. No point stays sharp forever; some need sharpening right out of the blister package.

Diamond, metal or ceramic hones should be used to sharpen hooks. Triangulated points with three cutting edges seem to be more effective than conical or needle-point types. And, it's easy to mash down or clip off the barb on most hooks. This leaves enough of a nubbin to hold the fish; yet, it makes it easier to un-hook fish without needlessly wounding them. Barbless hooks also improve the chances of releasing fish successfully.

The bend that creates the "gap" between the shank and the point is largely a matter of hook temper. A hook with a round bend seems less likely to snap than one with an acute angle bend, and the gap can be more easily enlarged without breaking the hook. Relatively soft-wire hook shanks bend easily. This is advantageous if it is caught in a snag or for imitating a bait's natural attitude in the water. Big-fish experts, however, insist on using large, heavy, forged hard-wire hooks that won't bend enough to release the fish during the fight.

Specialized hooks come in several configurations. Wide bend or Kahle hooks hold a live or dead minnow in a horizontal position beneath a bobber. Weedless hooks fitted with wire or fiber guards enable you to fish thick cover without snagging. Some double hooks have needle points or a separate shaft, so they can be inserted easily through the baits. Treble hooks, a favorite with some even though they disqualify bait catches from consideration for International Game Fish Association (IGFA) records, vary in size and gap. Many experts agree that single hooks work as well as trebles—even on lures. Partridge hooks, especially the specialty hooks developed for British bait anglers, deserve special attention; they seem better suited to bait fishing than the usual run of hooks. (They are rarely available in the United States, but are worth the search.)

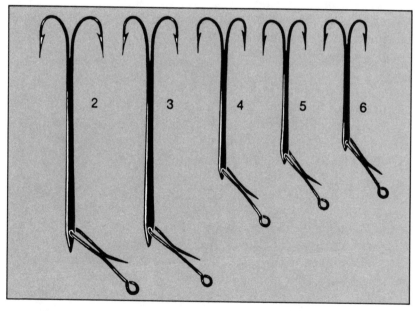

Among the many specialty hooks are these universal double bait hooks from Mustad. These hooks come in six different sizes, from 5/0 down to a No. 12 size.

Hooks, Sinkers And Floats

Hook finishes vary, too. Colored hooks like the Tru-Turns and some Japanese models come in reds, blues and greens. Color matters little when hooks are buried in your bait. Silver- or gold-finished hooks seem popular with salmon-egg buffs. Anglers who release deeply hooked fish by simply cutting the leaders should avoid corrosion-resistant finishes. The common bronze-finished hook rusts out faster. To avoid rusting in the tackle box, pack a desiccant, like baking powder or the commercial packaged material found in camera and electronic packaging, with your hooks. Hooks can be coated with a non-polluting rust-inhibiting spray to prevent rust, too. Put the hooks you remove during your fishing trip in a separate container; a film canister works well. Inspect, dry and resharpen these hooks after the trip at home before you return them to your ready tackle box.

Hook sharpening methods vary. Ceramic and diamond hones, sharpening stones and powered systems all work. However, the powered units give you a round, needle point. An inexpensive points file from an auto supply shop, which you can carry in your hat band, works, too. The trick to having sharp hooks is simple. A hook point that cuts in, rather than punches in, is easier to set. Therefore, bevel larger hooks so they are flat on the bottom of the bend and angled in on the sides to a sharp edge at the top, making the point triangular in shape. In the field, a few quick licks do the job in keeping your hooks sharp.

Picking The Right Sinker

Sinkers take the bait down to the depths where the fish lurk. The large number of different types and sizes shows their importance. As a rule, the lightest sinker offering both sufficient depth and, in combination with your bait, proper casting weight is the best choice. Some fish will take bait "on the drop" so a natural presentation works best. However, use a bigger weight to reduce "sink" time if fish are deep. In still water, use a sliding sinker that fish can't feel and the minimum amount of lead needed for effective trolling or ticking bottom in moving water.

Sinker-type depends upon the combination of method, bottom and water. For example, flat sinkers, such as pyramids, tend to stabilize in current. Disk-shaped sinkers offer an additional advantage in that they plane up over snags during the retrieve. Other stationary sinkers include split shot. Try the shot with

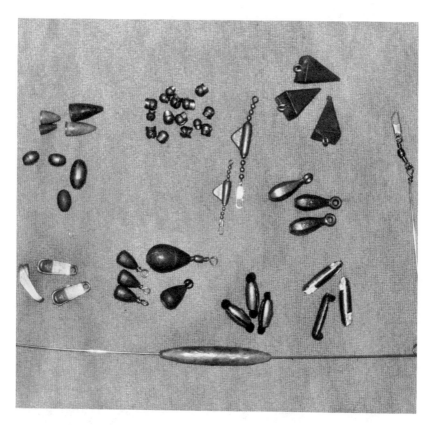

Fishermen can find sinkers for about any specific need. This array of sinkers ranges from bullet sinkers for fishing worms (top, left) to the walking sinker (lower right) used often in trolling.

"ears" as it's both reusable and soft enough so it won't crimp and weaken lines. Traditional bell or dipsey sinkers are a good choice for bottom fishing in still waters. Snap-Loc models are designed to snap on and off the line easily. Pinch-on and rubber-cored twist-on sinkers are popular, too. However, the use of sliding sinkers where fish are cautious or heavily pressured can make a major difference in your success rate.

To move the bait to the fish during trolling, specialized bead chain and keeled trolling sinkers work reasonably well. The Bait Walker and various other offset and wire-stem sinkers commonly used to reduce the number of snags in moving water also work well. In currents, all sorts of other options, such as surgical tubing and "pencil" lead, lead welding rods and soft wind-on leads, show the endless ingenuity of fishermen anxious to avoid hang-ups.

Hooks, Sinkers And Floats

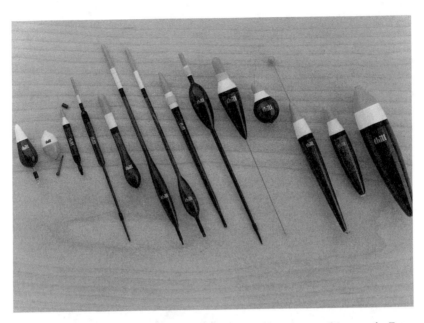

This commercial line of floats is patterned after floats which have been used for years by European fishermen. This approach raises American bobber fishing to a higher level.

Most of these work some of the time. Some, like the bullet sinkers designed for use in front of plastic worms, are major improvements over old favorites, such as egg sinkers, that hang up frequently. Throw-away sinkers, including tire balance weights, should be used in places where the bottom gobbles up substantial amounts of terminal tackle on a regular basis.

Sinkers and shot always get lost in tackle boxes. Stringing sinkers with eyes on a shower ring and carrying shot in a "frying pan" assortment, however, will maintain some order. For still-water applications, dipsey and walking sinkers rigged to slide above the swivel, leader and hook work well with minimum hardware. Buy an inexpensive mold, get some lead and you can easily cast at least a season's worth of most sinkers in an hour or so.

Call Them Floats, Not Bobbers

Only recently have Americans really embraced float fishing. Even fly fishermen have started using bobbers, although they call them "strike indicators" to overcome the Huck Finn image of bobber fishing. Bobbers, also known as floats, aren't universally popular. Some anglers complain that floats "blow about." However, you can fish floats and keep them relatively stable in even a strong wind by simply submerging the rodtip. Combining this technique with "pencil" or European-style floats, which are weighted so only the tip rides above water, makes the rig wind-proof. Wind can't move the line, nor can it move the float. With a proper bite indicator, even light bites are evident. Various bite indicators work, such as adding some foil to the line or using a commercial model that lights up or blows a whistle. Even a bell on the rodtip can bring you running when you've set out multiple lines.

Best of all, floats return control to the bait addict. With the proper float, you can set the correct depth and see the light bites. You can also place drift lines perfectly in moving water. All it takes is the right float and gear.

A few general rules bring order to float usage. First, the smaller the float, the better the result. Second, elongated floats are more sensitive than round floats because they can be pulled down with less effort. Third, floats need to be properly weighted according to their type and the presentation technique—meaning the indicator line just below the tip is even with the water surface. Fourth, color choices depend upon the water clarity, fish type and your eyesight. Dull colors suit sophisticated fish in clear water; bright, fluorescent colors are better for long distances and poor visibility situations. For extremely poor visibility or after dark, try lighted floats.

Floats come in fixed and sliding classes. Fixed floats usually are fastened to the line with rubber or plastic sleeves. Sliders which are ideal for casting have a stop at the greatest desired depth and a sinker and/or hook at the line's terminal end.

4

Basic Live-Bait Rigs

General rules for rigging should be considered before moving to specifics. In virtually all cases, the most natural presentation beats slavish imitation. The less weight that baits have to drag, the more natural their appearance. Lighter lines, smaller and lighter wire hooks and minimum-sized weights and floats make sense. Swivels that don't swivel and snaps, releases and other devices that serve mostly as an excuse for not tying new knots aren't really needed. Snelled hooks and commercial stop knots are not needed either.

What is needed is the simplest approach that allows your bait maximum movement and duration while hooked. This involves a careful study of a given bait's natural habitat. For example, consider grasshoppers in meadows, sculpin in fast, rocky streams, sawworms under elm trees or shrimp in tidal waters. Know where your baits normally live, and fish them where you catch them. You won't go wrong. It's also possible to do well with baits that are "out of place"—like using ghost shrimp, a marine species, for steelhead in rivers.

The "live" in live bait keys the action. The more natural, lifelike and succulent the appearance of the bait, the better the bite. This requires the best bait properly rigged and carefully presented in the right location at the right time.

Look Before Trying A New Bait
You can't properly rig a bait unless you know how it looks nat-

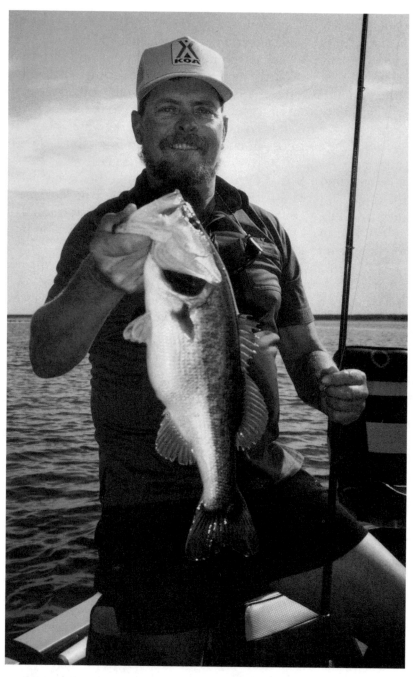

It can't get much more basic than this. A shiner fished under a bobber brought in this beauty. It was presented in a "natural" manner in order to fool the bass.

Basic Live-Bait Rigs   45

urally in the water. Start with a container full of water. A glass jar works; so does a small aquarium. Drop the bait you plan to use in or on the water. Check its motion, rate of descent and pattern of movement. Worms, for example, don't curl up into a ball with a little tag end. If you present worms in little, tight balls, savvy fish will depart. If trout hit nymphs swimming up to the surface, you want your bait to do the same. If you fish moving water, check to see what the bait does in current: Does it grab bottom? Does it drift near the top or burrow out of sight in the marl?

Sometimes, as in the case of minnows and other lively baits, use of an "injured" presentation may make the bait look more tempting. From a hungry fish's viewpoint, it looks more natural or at least like an easy meal. Hooking minnows upside down on jigs, forcing them to struggle to right themselves, and nipping off the ends of pectoral fins on Mad toms or bullheads that might use them to hold bottom can improve presentations. Shucking crayfish, if the soft "shedder" types aren't available, improves chances, too. Basically, predators, particularly large ones, want to ingest more calories from prey than the amount used to catch them. Baits that look "easy" work best!

So Many Choices

While some bait rigs work well in various conditions, most work best either in still or moving water, but not both. Baits can be presented either on the surface, subsurface or the bottom, and can either be static or moving. Fixed-depth rigs can offer either fixed depth from the surface or from the bottom. Variable-depth rigs, such as slip bobbers, can present baits "on the drop."

Add the lateral variable and the result is rigs designed to roll along stream courses or "hop" along lake bottoms. Other rigs can be trolled. With any given rig, you can and should vary the size of the hooks, sinkers and floats according to conditions. Sound confusing? It is, if you don't think before acting.

Still-Water Rigs

To fish water having little or no real current, you must understand the theory of the "sphere of discovery." This is the distance at which the fish first can see, sense or taste your bait. Think of your bait as a peach pit and the sphere of discovery as the peach skin. Slice the peach in half and the resulting half is "hemisphere

Expanding The Zone Of Discovery

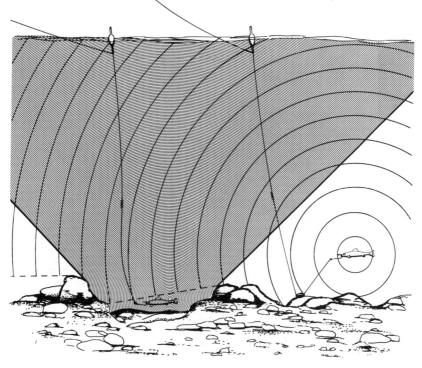

Fishing a bait a foot or so off the bottom instead of on the bottom has an advantage. The raised bait attracts fish from greater distances.

of discovery" for baits fished on the surface or bottom. If you cut most of the fruit away and jam the pit into a rocky-bottom crack, the sphere almost vanishes. If you float the pit a foot or so off the bottom, the area of water from which fish can be attracted to your bait radically increases. This is the reason air-injected worms or marshmallows work so well; they're a leader-length off bottom with a bigger discovery area.

Of course, if your bait's sphere of discovery sits in water that's too hot, too cold or, in the case of fish that stay put and ambush bait, too far from the right structure, you probably won't catch anything. There will be a difference in methods and movement around and on your favorite fishing water between species that cruise, like trout or salmon, and the more "stay at home" types, like muskies or bass, that ambush their prey.

Basic Live-Bait Rigs

In the first case, you can wait for the cruisers. Otherwise, try a few techniques or baits, then move to a new location if there isn't any action.

Topwater Presentations In Still Water

It's difficult to beat a simple hook on the end of a line for topwater presentations. Dapping, or dancing baits and flies on the surface, took fish for Izaak Walton. It still works today with frogs, moths and grasshoppers. A long rod or a telescopic pole rig does the job close in.

If you need casting range, try tying a casting bubble on the end of the line and add a leader that's 3 or 4 feet long for your hook and bait. Cast. Reel in slack and wait. This rig also works as a moving presentation. Add a dropper loop with a second bait about 2 feet above the bubble and retrieve slowly. Hybrid rigs, such as a small minnow on the terminal hook and a lively grasshopper on the dropper, are an advantage because they combine options.

Balloons aren't just for parties, either. They can help in situations where fish are rising out of casting range. Blow up the balloon to the maximum size desired—the bigger the balloon, the faster the drift in wind—and tie it off. Use a small rubber band or a very light breakaway leader to connect the balloon to the line. A dropper loop and hook or a double rig for one or two topwater baits completes the package. An air-injected, floating worm and a hopper are a good bait combination. The breakaway leader and rubber band prevent big fish from using the balloon's buoyancy to break light line.

In tidewaters and where pike and muskies lurk, you can substitute a popping cork for a casting float when fishing with frogs or big minnows. Sound seems to be an attraction, too. Big floating plugs or a stout hook on the cork are good insurance in case big fish hit the floats.

Subsurface Still-Water Options

From nymphs being fished just below the surface film to baits hanging just off bottom, subsurface presentations offer the most possibilities. Rigs with no lateral movement are either "on the drop," stationary or rising; "lateral movement rigs" are used by casters and trollers. The basic rig where bait weight is sufficient for casting is the simple terminal hook rig.

Balloons can be an effective piece of fishing tackle, as North American Fisherman Editor Steve Pennaz will readily attest. The balloon allowed the shiner to act naturally.

The classic "on the drop" bait is the terrestrial insect, worm or minnow fished without weight near the edges of weeds and other structure so it can slowly sink at a natural rate. Pole fishermen often use such rigs for panfish. If you can't cast an unweighted rig, place a small split shot a foot or so above the bait. If still more weight is needed, try a slip bobber rig. Thread on a slip bobber without the stopper. Add a stop, like a small swivel or a split shot, to the line end so the slip bobber won't jam the hook or snell. Then tie on the appropriate hook, bait it and cast the slip-bobber rig to the spot you want to fish. This offers maximum vertical coverage and works best off of specific structure, such as stumps, rocks or holes in weedbeds. Remember the drop speed is vital. Most fishermen use too much lead so the bait zooms past suspended fish. Very light, elongated bobbers with slip wire tie-ins on the top and bottom work better than the traditional bulky Styrofoam cork bobbers if their weight offers sufficient casting range. These bobbers show lateral movements and stops, indicating a fish has either mouthed or taken off with bait.

Working Mid-Depth, Still Water

Most American bait rigs suffer from a lack of depth control. You know your bait is on the bottom, but what is the depth? From spring until early winter, fish stay at particular depths which they find the most comfortable temperature-wise. Northern winters find most fish just under the ice or on or near the bottom.

As noted earlier, some fish cruise; others stay put. In either case, you will need to know the temperature preference of both the species and baitfish. Then find the depth at which that temperature occurs. By doing this, you eliminate a lot of "dead" water that only wastes valuable fishing time.

If you fish from the bank, you can only guess at the depth. If you go too shallow or too deep, you won't catch much. Have you ever been fishing from the bank with a whole batch of folks who are all using the same basic outfits and only one or two anglers are catching most of the fish? It's likely that their natural casting range puts them at exactly the right depth. However, the right bobber rig will help equalize these opportunities—even when fish are feeding on the bottom!

Float Rigs

The basic still-water rigger pinches on almost all split shot a foot above the bait, adds one large shot halfway between this shot bulk and the float and finishes up with a tiny shot 2 to 4 inches above the bait. The shots are adjusted so only the bright bobber tip appears above the surface. The tiny shot placed near the hook is really a bite indicator. When fish are biting lightly, they lift the bait so they feel only the weight of this tiny shot. You know you've got a bite because the bobber rises slightly in the water and points toward the fish.

Set the hook immediately by using a lateral movement of your rodtip away from the fish. This avoids the "slack first" problem otherwise faced with long rods. If you miss a couple of hits, increase the distance between your hook and the first bite-indicator shot to create a built-in delay. (The middle shot in this setup pre-

Utilizing A Wind-Beater Rig

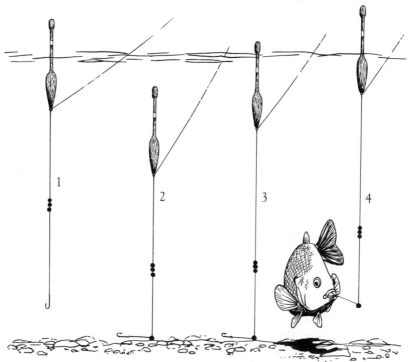

Positions 1, 2 and 3 show how to beat the wind with a weight near the bait. Position 4 is how a "bite on the rise" looks on the surface. Snap the rod in the direction the stem is leaning to set the hook.

vents the "bolo" tangles which might otherwise occur when the bobber and lead are rotating during the cast.) The graduated shot setup used for some moving water rigs is also a good choice for use in still water.

Don't let the wind hassle your bait, either. The British have a special, wind-proof bobber that is made with a long stem between the float and the small, spherical tip. European floats and some American-made bobbers are designed to ride beneath the surface with only the tip showing. Another key to beating the wind is as simple as using a submerged rodtip and rodtip rest. The rest can be easily made from a wire coat hanger. Cast out and submerge your rodtip. You can either hold it underwater or place it in your home-made rodtip rest so the tip remains submerged. After the rodtip is set in place, reel in slack line until the bobber barely moves. With no line and little bobber in the wind, your bait should stay in place. During a still-water bite, your bobber may submerge. More often, however, the float just tilts to one side or the other, or it may rise so it lies flat on the water. As a rule, set the hook at the first movement so that the fish doesn't swallow the hook.

This lift rigging—a "hair trigger" system—works over hard bottoms and is by far the best system for most heavily pressured gamefish that are both hook and weight shy. The basic still-water rig or, if windy, the windbeater system (outlined in the previous paragraph) can be modified by replacing the "bite-indicator" shot with a larger shot big enough to sink the bobber. The shot then rests on the bottom.

Setting the rig requires some fiddling. If the float sinks, reel it in a bit or place it farther from the sinker before your next cast. If the float lies on its side, make a longer cast next time or move the float a short distance toward the bait. When the rig's set properly, the float's tip will barely appear above the water when the rodtip is underwater. This maximizes the rod's sensitivity.

When fish nibble the bait, and big fish in heavy-pressure waters are extremely cautious feeders, they disturb the shot nearest the hook causing the bobber to rise toward the surface. Pull the rod free of the rests and set the hook immediately! This system seems to work particularly well early in the morning in waters where, during daylight hours, large numbers of fishermen pressure the fish with baits like salmon eggs, cheese or marshmallows. Big fish, as well as crayfish, seem to cruise in and fill up at night. If regulations permit fishing after dark, you can switch to a lighted bobber for going after these big cruisers.

While the previously mentioned rigs are effective at certain depths, some forage and, consequently, fish will be moving upward toward the surface. So, it's useful to fish a bait at various depths, such as 5, 15, 25 feet or even deeper on a single cast. The Biggie rig, the author's own creation, does this. Starting by threading the main line through the pointed end of a lead worm-head sinker, place either a bobber stop or tiny split shot about a foot above a dropper loop and hook setup that is 18 inches above a line-end bobber. It should be small enough so the worm sinker can still sink to the bottom. Then, bait the dropper loop hook and cast. Don't engage the baitcasting reel or close the spinning bail. Let the worm sinker go to the bottom; the bobber will rise to the top as the line travels freely through the sinker. When the bobber appears, close the bail, remove any slack in the line and place the rod in its rests. If you want to fish 5 feet below the surface, simply reel in 5 feet of line. If nothing much happens, reel in another 5 feet and try fishing at 10 feet. You can either pull line in a yard at a time or count the number of reel revolutions to obtain 5 feet. You can continue doing this until the bobber stop meets the worm sinker on the bottom. If you haven't lost count, you'll know the bottom's exact depth. If the bottom is too shallow, you can cast out farther or in a different direction next time.

You can reverse the system, too. After removing the slack, keep track of the amount of line reeled in until the bobber is at bottom—actually a foot off bottom. Start there and work back up in 5-foot increments until you find the depth where the fish are lurking! The Biggie system works with all natural baits. Of course, large minnows and frogs require large bobbers and weights; nymphs or worms lets you choose lighter gear. This is a unique system because it tells you exactly how deep you're fishing—even when fishing the steepest banks or over the most irregular bottoms!

Bottom Rigs

The standard bottom rig with the sinker on the end of the line and 2-foot-long droppers and hooks 18 inches apart takes fish over hard bottoms whether you lower your terminal tackle down the side of a piling or rock wall or your bait touches the bottom. Modifications include umbrella-type wire rigs used to spread perch baits, such as minnows, over a wider area. However, various sliding sinker rigs make good sense, especially when combined with baits such as air-injected worms which seem to become more visible to fish. Or, replace the terminal bobber on the Biggie rig with a hook and go for it!

Many different sinker shapes have been developed to make this basic rig work differently. The shoehorn-shaped sinker of the Lindy Rig, the pyramid sinkers designed for sand, flat no-snag sinkers that plane up over snags on the retrieve, sinkers with swivels to reduce line twist and others of different design all will work. "Minimum density" sinkers, however, deserve special mention. You can make these by sticking lead-rod sinkers through Styrofoam balls. The objective is a sinker that is heavy enough to cast but will barely sink. Thus, it sits on top of deep weeds and muck and can both improve bait visibility and reduce hang-ups.

Except for casting floats that are slowly reeled in to cover more water, all of the previously mentioned methods offer intensive coverage of a small area, such as a treetop or other confined structure. When prospecting, however, you need rigs that let you move the bait.

Moving-Water Rigs

Current that takes the scent of your bait downstream helps you enjoy several alternatives. You can still fish and let the fish come to you, such as when catfishing. This also seems a reasonable alternative for migratory fish, such as steelhead or salmon. You can also let your bait move downstream to fish that aren't actively feeding. To be successful, however, you must be able to stay out of the fish's view and know where given species feed and rest.

Topwater baits, such as an air-injected worm or grasshopper, can be fished with just a single hook. In most cases, you need casting weight. A conical translucent casting bobber at the end of the line allows you to use a dropper to dap and float baits that might not stay up on their own. (If you use very small minnows hooked just ahead of the dorsal fin so the minnow "flutters" near the surface, you may discover a smallmouth or brown trout hiding in a favorite stream.) This is also an excellent method after dark. The rig is simple: A foot-long snell to the bait set 3 feet above the bobber minimizes snagging on the cast.

Rigging a 2- or 3-foot-long snell below the bobber allows you to present delicate baits, such as insects, over picky fish that might spook at the sight or shadow of the bubble. It's important to hold back on the float so the bait gets there first.

Mid-Depth Rigs For Moving Water

Only floats allow you to fish mid-depths consistently. The type of bobber you use, as well as the rigging method, depends upon the water's depth and speed. In very shallow streams, ultralight gear, a round bobber that is contained by a shot above it and a bait and mini-shot on the terminal (hook) end lets you fish even over moss.

Moving-water bobbers vary considerably compared to stillwater types. These bobbers have the flotation near the top for better control. Thick "chubs" move minnows and amphibians nicely.

Maintaining Proper Bait Placement

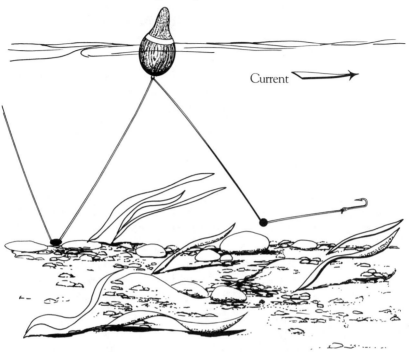

Current ➛

Placing a large split shot above the float in shallow, flowing water causes the float to drift more slowly than the bait. This allows the bait to reach the fish first.

Thinner stick and antenna rigs handle lighter baits. Self-cocking bobbers with wire stems or standard bobbers with the shot nipped on at the stem work better with baits that need to be presented just under the water's surface film.

Most fishermen don't vary their terminal rigs enough when water depth and currents change, or they move or cast to different spots. Tiny differences in sinker weights can make the difference between taking fish and not taking fish. Add or subtract small shot so baits tick bottom every now and then. Stop! Don't pinch shot onto your main line; even if you use soft shot, this action will weaken the line and may cause a break-off. Instead, split shot pinched on a doubled line section and slid on over the line between two small shot—called a sliding shot dropper—reduces possible loss of terminal tackle and is less damaging to the line itself.

When you hang up, in most cases, you'll lose only part of the shot on the doubled monofilament, so it's easy to replace. If the entire double-line section pulls off, prepared anglers merely thread a pretied double-line shot string between two small shot at the line end. You can also increase the grip of individual shot by making a loop in the line and crimping the shot down on the loop's double strand so there's less chance of weakening your line.

If you must pinch shot on your line, put it at the end of the line and run a dropper or a long snell with your bait. Then, when the shot snags or the line breaks where it has been pinched, you will most often save your hook and bait. This isn't a bad ultra-light rig for still-water fishing, either.

The more swivels, snaps, sinkers and other adornments you hang on the line, the more likely a tackle-eating snag. So, in moving water, you can use the double-line split shot system up to about ½ ounce in weight. When you need more weight, a piece of surgical tubing with a section of wire works well. The only problem with this is wasting pieces of lead from trimming when fine-tuning the drift rigs. Save the pieces for sinker casting, pound them flat for use as pinch-on sinkers or use less lead than needed, leaving a tubing "tail" to crimp split shot to the tail.

On smooth bottoms, you can use a standard fish-finder rig with a sliding sinker. This allows you to position the sinker in a prime drift pattern and, by paying out line, move your bait downstream. This assumes, of course, that you are using a bait large enough so that the current drag on the bait and the line up to the sinker is greater than the current's drag on the line from the sinker to where it leaves the water. If not, the line will bag or move ahead of the bait creating unwanted slack. Dipsey and round sinkers that roll usually snag less often than other shapes.

Bobbers that are positioned so the bait "ticks" bottom every 15 to 30 seconds also reflect bottom action because you see exactly where your bait is working. That's why this rig is favored by steelhead guides who can easily see if a client's drift is off-line. Bobbers also carry the bait directly downstream in productive currents because the bobber's bulk counteracts the current's lateral pull which would carry the bait into slack water.

On stream bottoms of fairly uniform depth, the shot needed to sink the bobber to its mark can be evenly spaced from small shot near the hook to large shot toward the bobber. When working

Double-Line Shotting System

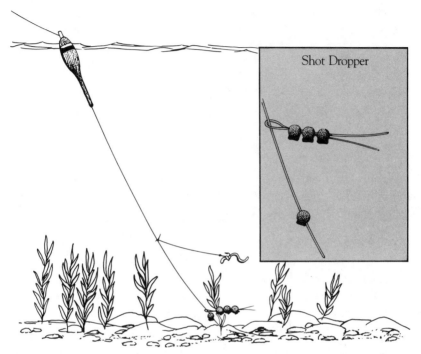

Shot Dropper

The double-line shotting system (right) prevents loss of numerous hooks and bait on snaggy, tackle-eating bottoms. The shot is attached to the main line (left) so only the shot is lost in a snag.

over very uneven bottoms, rig a single small shot 6 inches above the bait and the bulk of the shot about a foot higher. Add one large shot midway between bait and bobber to prevent tangles resulting from the "bolo" effect created when a bobber is rigged a long way from the bait. This rig makes it easy to change depth; just move the bobber and the anti-tangle shot.

Moving-water bites sometimes will submerge the bobber. More often, however, large fish merely stop the bobber's drift or the bobber moves an inch or two cross-current. When this happens, raise your rodtip and, if you feel a fish, move the rod laterally to set sharp, thin wire hooks.

Minnows reveal when gamefish are chasing them by the bobber action. The constant swing and sway of a sensitive bobber also tells you whether the minnow is frisky or about to expire.

Basic Live-Bait Rigs

Slip-Bobber Rig

This setup keeps bait close to a fairly level bottom. It also works on uneven bottoms because the bait's depth can be changed quickly by moving the bobber and middle shot up or down.

Basic Bobber Choices

Whether fishing in still or moving water, bobber choice is more critical than most anglers think. Forget the typical red and white globe bobber! It is too insensitive and fragile for most fishing applications. With long, slender bobbers, it is much easier to spot bites. Even wine corks pressed into service as bobbers work better than the familiar globes!

With large baits, such as minnows and suckers. the hollow, clear-plastic, conical bobbers with a screw eye at each end work well. You can either tie the line onto the skinny end and fasten a leader at the fat end or run the line through each eyelet to the terminal tackle. Rubber bands looped around the bobber will hold the line in place. Simply pull line under the rubber bands to vary the depth.

Staying Attached

It's easy to attach long, thin bobbers; just string inch-long pieces of rubber tubing on the line. In still water, the bobber should be attached only at the bottom so it is stabilized in wind. In moving water, the bobber should be attached at the bottom if the wind is blowing downstream. This will keep the bobber in the main current. If the wind is blowing upstream, attach the bobber at both ends and spray dry-fly flotation liquid on the first 20 feet of line so it floats. Then the wind will hold back the bobber so the bait goes downstream first. When not using floats, string on extra sections of tubing that slide up and down the line. To complete your bobber rig you need sharp light wire hooks small enough to be hidden in live bait such as crayfish, maggots, worms, minnows and other baits that attract fish through movement, taste and scent. Light wire provides a more natural action; these hooks can be bought in well-stocked fly-fishing shops.

Once your outfit is properly rigged, you need to find a good spot, like a rocky riffle. Slow, long pools that are a bit too deep to wade in are particularly attractive. Just adjust your bobber-to-bait distance so the bait suspends near the bottom. The bobber will lie on its side. If the split shot sinkers rest on the bottom, shorten the bobber-to-bait distance. Watch your bobber closely because you will catch more fish than ever before!

Worms And Leeches

5

Worms Of All Kinds

Charles Darwin's book *The Formation of Vegetable Mould, Through the Action of Worms, with Observations on Their Habits* shows the importance of worms as soil builders. Clearly, worms deserve their billing as America's most popular live bait. As with leeches, worms are always available commercially, and could not be easier to catch and keep. The puzzle is why do fish take worms so readily? Except for a few marine species, like pile worms, worms aren't aquatic. Only when rains sweep worms into muddy streams do these wigglers become aquatic. Maybe fish see them as a seasonal delicacy, like strawberries. For whatever reason, worms work.

With over 1,000 species to select from, anglers enjoy a wide range of choices. Small red worms are just big enough to entice panfish. Nightcrawlers tempt bass. Texans might want to import Australian earthworms that grow to 10 feet in length and over an inch in diameter! An import, the African nightcrawler, is earthworm size, but it's so lively that it will crawl out of uncovered beds. It's a deservedly popular panfish bait where available.

Worm confusion compounds with names. Even the most common earthworm—Helodrilus caliginosus—lurks under a variety of nom de plumes, such as garden hackle or fish worms. Regional varieties, such as the Southern grunt worm, abound. Common names seem too confusing; scientific names too difficult to remember. Therefore, big ones are nightcrawlers and little ones are "worms."

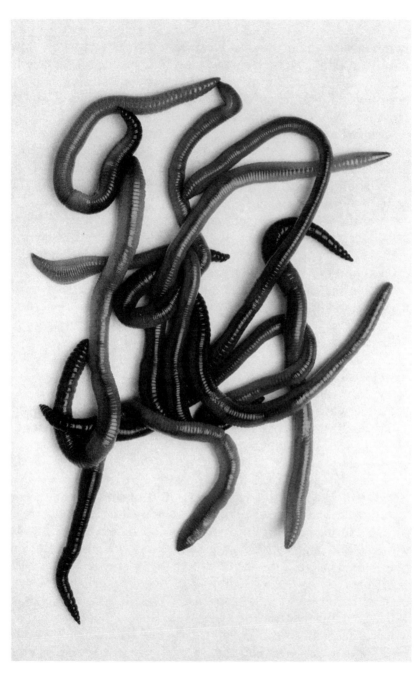

Nightcrawlers probably are the most popular bait of all the worm species. Though there may be strong regional favorites, nightcrawlers have an almost universal appeal because of their size and active nature.

Worms Of All Kinds

Worms can be divided into three basic classes: earthworms, nightcrawlers and manure and leaf worms. Sizes vary wildly from massive nightcrawlers that may top 10 inches and are ready to freeline for big bass down to tiny red wiggler worms, a popular Southern panfish bait that also works well on trout. Wigglers might average 2 inches in length.

Earthworms, the proletarian fellows found everywhere, run 3 to 4 inches in length with all sorts of terra-cotta color variations and a few oddments such as bright red or an off-blue tint.

Nightcrawlers, the domestic types, run larger with lengths up to 10 inches.

Manure worms, like their more bucolic cousins the leaf worm and the featherweight, domesticated red wiggler, tend to be firm and lively. Leaf worms seem a bit stouter with a flattened tail. But it's doubtful that fish can tell the difference.

However, the worm's appeal to fish seems to depend more upon size and texture; texture, like color, depends upon selection, rearing conditions and habitat. Size is also critical; shorter worms seem to be the choice of panfish and other "nibblers."

The Worm's World

Worms thrive in loose loam because it is easy for them to digest their way through it. A worm is a long, hollow digestive organ that eats its weight every 24 hours. The worm's excrement or "cast" is, as Darwin noted, incredibly valuable for fertilizing and enriching the soil.

Even though worms lack eyes and ears, they can sense and avoid light and vibrations by using primitive sensory cells. As a result, those who would stalk nightcrawlers after dark must tread softly and tote a dim flashlight. Worms, although primitive, are widespread. Damp earth in shade remains optimum habitat, but some worm species can survive in acid, sandy or even rocky soil.

Worms reproduce incredibly fast. Even though a worm has both male and female sex organs, it can't fertilize itself. So worms will lie head-to-tail to fertilize each other's eggs. A cocoon, or sac, will drop from the worm's collar; baby worms hatch in two or three weeks and mature in six months. Worms all regenerate body parts; some even double if sliced in half. However, many bifurcate worms will die if cut in half; so, this is a risky way of trying to double your worm supply!

Popular Types Of Worms

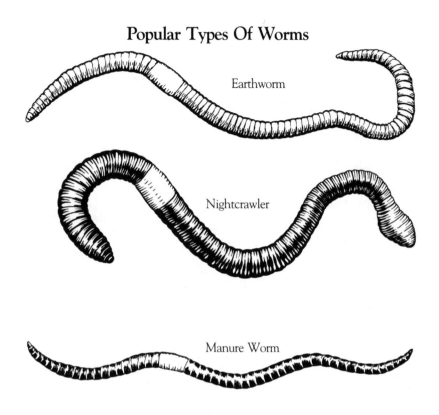

Earthworm

Nightcrawler

Manure Worm

Three popular types of earthworms are the standard earthworm (top), the nightcrawler (middle) and the manure worm (bottom). All will draw fish.

In the spring, it's quite easy to collect more than enough worms for a season's fishing. You don't even have to worry about keeping them all alive—dead worms work as bait, too. If you freeze some of your worms in water in ice cube trays, you will have emergency bait during the summer. It's probably wise, however, to have a separate garage refrigerator for the bait.

Gleaning worms for bait use is a great way to introduce small children to fishing.

Earthworms aren't difficult to dig out if the soil is reasonably damp and loose. Be sure you don't waste time and energy digging in soil that has been treated to prevent worms. Golf courses and smooth, elegant lawns usually are treated. Try grassy areas that are a bit irregular as a result of hardened worm cast on the surface. Good garden soil, like flower or vegetable beds, also should hold lots of worms. A bed soaked well in the afternoon should have worms waiting in the top foot of soil the next morning. Don't shovel; that guillotines the bait. Dishwater can be used as a chum for worms; pour some on an out-of-the-way spot in the yard and cover it with a few boards. Nutrients in the dishwater attract worms up under the boards where they're easily dug. Worms usually will be lurking right underneath a heavy mulch or a plastic sheet used to control weeds.

Lawn-watering or heavy rains induce nightcrawlers to leave their burrows to prowl about sidewalks and streets. You can pick up many worms right off the pavement. If you're reluctant to handle them, they can be flipped into a box with a spatula. More conservative nightcrawlers will be only partly exposed, so grab these lightly at ground level and hold them until they tire. Then they can be pulled from their holes. Pull hard, and you have half a worm! Conservative nightcrawlers are easier to spot in areas with short grass, such as untreated golf courses or park lawns.

If you don't like a lot of digging, simply lay a piece of felt carpet (foam-backed carpet won't work) over a patch of shady ground that has been dug up and kept wet. Let it lie a few days, then roll off the carpet and pick up both nightcrawlers and lob or dew worms. Soaking walnut shells in a couple of gallons of water for several days also works. Dump the dark walnut water on the ground. The walnut's natural tannin seems to irritate worms, forcing them up onto the surface. After rinsing the worms in some clean water quickly, they're ready to use. Other more caustic chemicals work; however, they aren't recommended because they pollute the ground and drive away the worms.

The biggest nightcrawlers available are sought by those who hunt "hawg" bass or trophy pike. Eight- to 10-inch-plus worms offer a special appeal for big fish; however, such worms can be difficult to find. One angler solved the problem by organizing neighborhood "worm derbies." Local small fry could win a prize for the biggest trophy nightcrawler and receive a penny a worm for anything over 6 inches found after every rain.

Leaf And Manure Worms

Leaf worms hide in leaf mold and are easily found by raking wet, rotting leaves. One type, the Southern grunt worm, prefers pine woods and acid soil. A method for collecting the grunt worm

Bloodworms are a popular bait in saltwater and brackish water. They also can be used in freshwater, especially when steelhead fishing. Bloodworms can be cut in sections to fit small hooks.

is unusual, but it works. Drive a stake into moderately damp ground and rub an axe or a piece of steel on the head of the stake. Worms pop up in an effort to avoid the unpleasant vibrations. Other odd methods of worm collection include the use of low voltage electrical rods in damp ground (*not* recommended) and various chemical solutions, including a mix of 10 percent mustard and water, that will usually bring leaf worms up top. However, it's probably quicker to just fork up the worms in soft soil.

Manure worms are found under old manure piles. Fresh piles, like fresh compost piles, are too hot for worms. Another good spot is around sewage treatment plants.

Mini-Munchies For Small Fish

Red wigglers, a commercial worm species grown in the South,

offer considerable advantages for trout and panfishermen working under tough conditions. However, the same-sized immature "gray" nightcrawlers raised in a mix of sand and peat work even better because they are more lively. Sometimes, however, they can be difficult to impale on a hook.

Clearly, small worms take more small fish. Worms should fit easily into the quarry's mouth. The use of standard nightcrawlers for bluegills, for example, will result in lots of nibbles but few hooked fish—unless the angler uses nightcrawler pieces. You can also bait with half a worm.

Marine Worms

Several marine worms seem to be binders between leeches and true worms. As with terrestrial worms, pile-, sand- or bloodworm nomenclature reflects habitat or appearance. These worms work in salt and brackish water and, not surprisingly, seem effective for anadromous fish, like steelhead, in freshwater.

Pile worms, ignoring the worm's capability to give the unwary angler a nasty nip with its pincher mouth, are extremely tough. Threading a pile worm onto a 6X long-shank hook so it can slide up the snell when a fish hits can catch a dozen saltwater panfish with the same worm. These worms live among mussels and other shellfish on pilings and seawalls. These worms are easily collected if you use a geologist's pick or pry bar. Sand and blood worms come from sand or mud bottoms around clam beds or ghost and other burrowing shrimp.

Care And Handling Of Bait Worms

Worms kept cool and damp can survive two or three months in a commercial bedding material or a homemade mix of half shredded newspaper and half leaf mold. If worms dry out, they will die. Therefore, if you're buying worms from a commercial outlet, you should always check their quality. Worms from local bait shops or the ubiquitous rural worm magnate operating behind a "Worms For Sale" sign normally are in better shape than those purchased from a retail chain outlet.

If you can, choose the lively worms over the couch potatoes. Rinse the worms, if possible, so you can better see that they are in good condition. (This also saves time on the water because you won't have to grade worms when you should be fishing.) Most quality worm outlets sell well-conditioned worms that are fatter and larger than average. You can also condition worms yourself in a day or so. What's most important is that their texture is firm and, of course, that they are the proper size for the fish you're seeking. Generally, you can improve worm texture by storing them for several weeks in damp—not sopping wet—sand.

Whether you buy or glean worms, investing in worm containers makes sense. Commercial cardboard containers are okay for a short time period. Lay some strips of wet paper on top of the worms, then put some weight on the top. The worms will absorb the water and expand in size.

Many expert anglers use two containers. A basic, insulated container, like a commercial worm box or a homemade Styrofoam box, works well. During hot weather, insert either a plastic container of ice or a refreezable pack so worms neither drown in excess water from the ice melt nor cook in the sun. You should place the worm container on a cushion or pad in your car or pickup when driving to the water; excess vibrations can kill worms.

Ready containers need not be fancy. Tin cans work, but they are easier to use if a wire is attached in holes punched near the top of the can. A tobacco tin also works nicely if you punch air holes in the cover. Such tins also slide easily into a pocket or vest for carrying when your hands are full of gear. On very hot days, place a well-rinsed, soaked kitchen sponge in the container lid. A flip-flop, metal, belt-mounted bait container works exceptionally well as a ready box for stream fishermen. It can be restocked with a dozen or more worms as needed. Damp sphagnum moss works nicely in such containers and wet, shredded newspaper works in a pinch. The moss has the added benefit of improving the worm's texture; it tends to scour out any ingested dirt. As a result, the worms are tougher and more lively, too.

Another effective way to tote worms is in corrugated cardboard rolls. Tear the smooth, outer layer off one side of a 5-by-15-inch piece of corrugated cardboard and place a few worms on the cardboard. Most will slide immediately into the slots while the others can be pushed in. Moisten the cardboard slightly and roll it up; store the rolled cardboard in a sealable plastic bag or a tin container with a lid. Worms will remain happy all day. As you need bait, simply unroll the cardboard. A few pieces of cardboard in the traditional flip-top tobacco can works, too.

Two types of worm containers sold at most bait shops are foam coolers (top) with lids and containers that can be opened from both sides (bottom).

Presorting worms by size saves time on the water. To customize your bait to your hook size, it's worthwhile to sort your bait into several ready containers. Tote a container of 2- to 3-inch worms for stream trout or bluegills, another for 4- or 5-inch worms for crappies and a third with your biggest nightcrawlers for larger gamefish.

A worm's color seems to make a difference in some water conditions. In clear water, for example, the choice seems to be very well-conditioned, almost translucent worms. If some purists are correct, fish can distinguish among colors, so you might want to produce your own "technicolor" worms. Adding brick dust to the worms' storage bed creates "really red" worms. For other colors, saturate your storage container with various vegetable dyes.

Many anglers believe such bright-colored worms can help in clear water. Even with a light bobber rig, you'll see some bites only when the bright worm disappears as it's nipped by a fish. Following drifts when freelining worms is much easier if a bright-colored worm is used, too.

Whether the worms were gleaned and raised or purchased in bulk and saved until needed, large containers filled with commercial worm bedding or a homemade mix of good loose soil and leaf mold enables you to keep worms for months. A worm pit can be as simple as a box or frame lined with a mesh or wood set into soft ground in a shady spot. Replace the soil once a year. A lid conserves moisture and keeps active worms, like African nightcrawlers, in and local animals and birds out.

In areas subject to frozen ground or rocky or clay soil, consider using above-ground containers, such as half-wine barrels or boxes. Almost anything works as a container, although metal containers should be painted inside and out so they won't rust out. Don't forget to provide screened drainage holes in the bottom of your worm farm so the worms don't drown! Be sure metal and other above-ground boxes are protected from direct sunlight and from freezing. Straw mulch also helps protect worms in below-ground boxes that are subject to frigid temperatures.

Fill the box with commercial worm mix or simply layer in sod

Building A Worm Farm

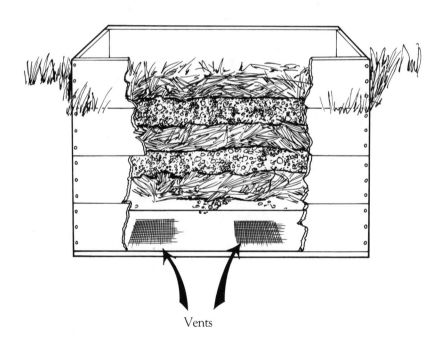

Vents

Worm farms need screen-covered holes in the bottom to allow excess water to drain. This prevents the worms from drowning. The box should also be buried in dirt so the worms won't freeze or overheat.

or leaf mold with friable (crumbled) soil. Wait long enough to ensure the worm bedding doesn't compost and warm the material past 50 degrees, causing them to die. Then, add about 50 nightcrawlers or 150 earthworms per cubic foot. The next day remove any dead or dying worms and chop, freeze and use them for chum. Keep the growth container moist, but not wet.

It takes about two months for worms to reproduce and four to six months for their offspring to reach full-size. With good management, each cubic foot of soil will produce 1,000 to 2,000 redworms and 300 to 500 nightcrawlers a year.

Feeding the worms isn't difficult. Every two months blend a mix of ½ cup lard and 2 cups cornmeal into the top 2 inches of dirt. It's easy to see the yellow meal; when the yellow disappears, it's time to feed again. Some worm growers use a split grapefruit, placing it cut-side down on top of the worm bedding. When the soft pulp disappears, it's time for more. Use caution when feeding; overfeeding kills more worms than underfeeding.

Desperate anglers who have run out of their worm supplies when the first spring rains are coloring the waters and the fish are gobbling worms can often find worms near streams, around dead and decaying wood and under stumps. Carry a few sealable plastic bags to hold such baits of opportunity. Having a trowel or shovel handy sure helps. Digging worms on the stream bank itself is not beneficial to the riparian habitat or the stream's water quality. It's not recommended.

Basic Worm-Rigging Methods

Basic worm rigs depend upon the quarry species, the habitat and the worm size. In moving water, worms naturally appear following rainstorms, so fishing with worms when water starts to "color up" always produces. Worms also seem natural in meadow streams that cut through deep loam; leaf worms, in particular, appear natural in streams in forested areas. Spending a few minutes poking around under fallen trees and turning over rocks can fine-tune your selection.

All popular plastic-worm rigs, such as jig heads, Texas or Arkansas rigs and various multi-hook harnesses, work even better for those who cast nightcrawlers. Systems with the hook point exposed offer a better chance of clean hooksets. However, weedless methods in which the hook point and barb are buried offer obvi-

Complete Angler's Library

Favorite Worm Riggings

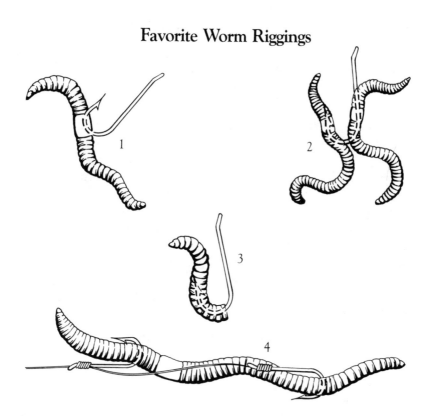

When rigging worms, they are usually hooked through the collar (1). For added attraction, two worms can be put on one hook (2) and, in fishing for panfish, a piece can be used (3). For trolling, a double-hook rig (4) works well.

ous advantages in heavy cover where snags are common.

Hooks with longer shanks designed for worms improve presentations in situations where either the bait or the water is moving and you want the worm fully extended. Plastic-worm hooks with barbs in the head help hold worms on hooks. Tru-Turns and other bent hooks that rotate in the fish's mouth seem to offer a better barb set than in-line hooks. Very light wire hooks or, where extra casting weight is needed without the use of shot, heavy short shank hooks, like a Siwash, are well-suited for dead drop and bobber systems.

Moving Water. The best rig for most conditions is simple: a single hook inserted through a portion of the worm's collar and, if possible, fished unweighted. This method requires careful assessment of currents, upstream casting with ultra-light gear or a sim-

This is a more secure way to attach a worm to a hook. The ends are still free to wiggle, and you have a better chance of catching those "nibblers" that never want to commit themselves.

ple downstream drift. It's easy on brooks and small streams but is nearly impossible on big water. A floating fly line with a 6- or 7½-foot leader towing a No. 8 hook and a worm is tough to beat for species like trout. (Add split shot above the hook only if completely necessary.)

A long rod with its rodtip submerged, a short line and a worm, plus some very aggressive wading, allow you to fish pockets around boulders in white water that most anglers miss. In slow-moving streams, bobbers shine by elongating the bait's natural drift and keeping worms out of reach of bottom-dwelling critters, like crayfish.

Still-Water Worms. In still water, worms simply sink to the bottom. If you want a swimming presentation to cover more water, hook up a leech or fish inlets having current. Imitating natural sink rates can be important when fish are finicky. A wire-stemmed bobber that cocks vertically without weight and rides above a leader holding a collar-hooked worm just off the bottom replicates nature best. Slip bobbers work best at depths that exceed the length of the rod. Fixed British-style bobbers work better in the shallows. Attach Texas- and Carolina-style worm rigs with nightcrawlers for bass or pike; however, use smaller hooks on very light tackle with 3- to 4-inch-long angleworms for panfish or small trout. Both rigs work alone, as well as with floating jigs and air-injected worms.

In some cases, the obvious worm-head weight just won't do the job. If this happens, consider using a weighted hook. A bit of solder on the shank is one solution; a wrap of glued-down, lead wire is another. Both systems help hold the worm in place.

Bridge Bobbers. You can also fasten a large bobber—a big, clunky model in Styrofoam works as long as it's heavy enough to cast—to the end of your line with a slip knot or split shot that will let the float pull free if it snags. Add a dropper leader and worm 3 to 5 feet above the bobber. If the Styrofoam float casts like an empty coffee cup, insert a lead rod or glue on a sinker that's just heavy enough for the foam to barely float. You can also use a conical casting bobber.

This rig is designed to be fished with the line riding on the water and the bobber resting in the weeds or on the bank. Toss the float past the hole in the weeds or on the bank. If properly done, the dropper-rigged worm will dangle within a clear pocket in the weeds or next to the snag that's impossible to cast to. By moving up or down the bank or around in your boat, you can place the worm exactly in the right place to tempt fish—even in awkward, hard-to-reach spots.

This rig also works for dapping insects and other baits. Use the heavy line necessary to haul out the big fish. (Dropper leader length will vary to reflect the needed bobber-to-dropper and dropper-to-bait distances. Be sure that the bobber-to-dropper length is at least a foot shorter than the dropper-to-hook length so the line doesn't tangle during the cast.)

6

Leeches Enchant Fish

U pper Midwest fishermen lust after leeches that catch walleyes, bass, trout, panfish and other species. You can buy or catch leeches almost anywhere, and, from time to time, various sporting types talk of "outlawing" leeches that, in the hands of a growing school of experts, "endanger" smallmouth populations.

Throughout the rest of the country, however, leeches are not that popular. So, if you want to use what many experts consider the finest warm-water bait for most gamefish, you need to catch your own leeches. With gamefish limits in mind, it's easy to ward off caustic comments about blood suckers and Dracula's baby. Fortunately, no live bait is as easy to catch and keep as the lusty leech.

Leeches are found in most still or slow-moving waters, and are quite common in farm ponds or ditches carrying few gamefish. Finding large numbers of leeches, therefore, indicates an absence of gamefish. Most often leeches will anchor with one sucker and wait for targets of opportunity with their sucker mouth. When leeches swim, they look like sidewinder rattlesnakes.

Leeches haven't had much respect since the so-called medicine leech, a species of the larger class of bloodsuckers that use teeth to gnaw through skin and suck the blood and tissue, dropped out of the medical business when doctors gave up on blood letting as a common cure-all. At their best, leeches offer a lively wiggle, a tough texture and a major attraction for most gamefish.

Leeches are a great summer bait because they survive in warm,

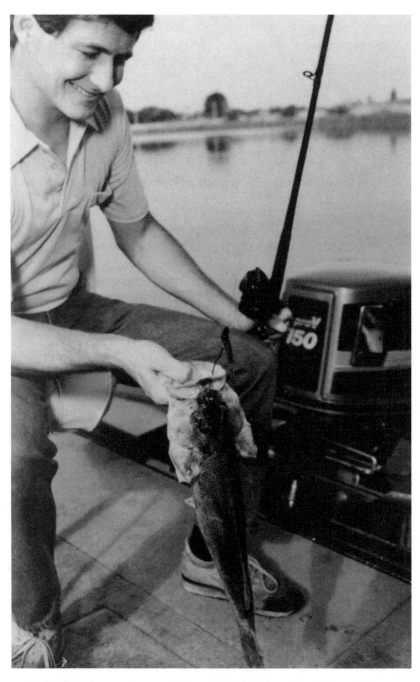

Leeches bring satisfaction to many anglers—not just bass fishermen but walleye and other major gamefish anglers, too. A bent-shank hook improves the chances of a solid hook-up.

Leeches Enchant Fish

even downright hot, water. In fact, they only work well in water temperatures above 50 degrees. If the water temperature is below 50, you should switch to minnows or worms. (Leeches ball up on the hook. It's an attempt, apparently, to conserve body heat.)

Leeches collected early in the spring easily survive a summer's deprivation in your bait container.

Ribbon Leeches

Leeches vary in size and some are more lively than others. The most common commercial type available, the ribbon leech, suits the palates of larger gamefish, such as bass and trout.

Color isn't a reliable identifying mark. For example, ribbon leeches vary from tan to black and some have spots. However, good bait leeches all share one characteristic: They vigorously wiggle and squirm when you try to hold them.

Ribbon leeches can be distinguished from similar looking horse leeches by texture. Bait leeches are firmer. Also, horse leeches are easy to spot because they have an orange underbelly and red dots on the back.

Even though ribbon leeches are the commercial choice, local species will work if they are firm and frisky. Don't cull them out simply because they're different. However, local species, like horse leeches, may repel gamefish because of their unattractive scent. You may also discover that a certain species from a local stream or pond may be so good that less successful anglers will start clamoring to have them outlawed. (This was the case with ribbon leeches that were used for smallmouth fishing.)

Tiger Leeches

Tiger leeches weren't always considered good bait. They are small and extremely lively, making it difficult to put them on a hook. Then a few experiment-minded bait fishermen discovered they were dandy baits for trout and panfish. Even though tigers (their name stems from the row of spots down the back) are smaller than ribbon leeches, they wiggle more rapidly and are exceptionally durable in fast-moving, summer trout waters. These lively leeches are a cure for the "lockjaw" that larger gamefish occasionally develop, too. Even when bass or pike are too stuffed to gobble another minnow, they will suck up snacks like a small tiger leech or a maggot.

Tiger leeches—those with spots on the back—are a popular bait. Even though they tend to be smaller than other leech species, their liveliness is a major plus in catching fish.

Leeches—Gathering, Care And Maintenance

Preserving leeches is as easy as stashing them in buckets in a bait refrigerator. Side-by-side coolers—one for leeches, the other for minnows—on the top shelf with room for other baits below offers an ideal setup.

A season's worth of leeches can also be stored in an inexpensive, water-filled Styrofoam cooler placed in a cool, shaded spot. Divide the storage containers in half with a window screen to separate ribbon and tiger leeches, or large and small leeches. It's much easier to segregate them in the comfort of your garage than in a boat.

Wide-mouth, gallon glass jars filled with water work, too. Half-gallon plastic milk cartons hold fewer leeches; however, they pack so well in the refrigerator that you may be able to store more

Leeches Enchant Fish

bait in them than in larger, bulkier containers. Using several small containers also makes it easier to determine when any leeches turn suckers up. If kept in clean, unchlorinated water under 50 degrees and checked once a week to remove dead and dying specimens, leeches caught in the spring should survive all summer without food. (They just shrink a bit.) Feeding small amounts of sliced liver to the leeches will head off this shrinkage, but some feel the enforced fast improves the leeches' texture. Also, because they're hungry, they seem to wiggle more vigorously on the hook.

Remember that chlorine kills leeches, so use unchlorinated water, such as rainwater or well water, or buy pills at the pet store to remove chlorine. At the end of the season, return the leftover leeches to their pond.

Spring is the best time to gather leeches because of the large number of "pre-spawn" adults. In the warm waters of summer, leech numbers decline because adults die after leaving the cocoons that hold the next year's leech population. Summer collection is possible, but just not that productive in most waters. This is why it's difficult to store leeches at home during winter.

Good collection spots for leeches include farm ponds, backwaters, ditches and other waters heavily overgrown with shoreline vegetation. Keys to finding large leech populations include a big summer algae bloom, the absence of gamefish and a little current to spread the scent of decomposing bait.

Many anglers look for leeches in ponds with large populations of fathead minnows. The minnows die in the spring after spawning, providing copious leech fodder. Again, the best spots within such habitat include places where a slight current moves the smell of your bait to leeches. Double up with crayfish or minnow traps and collect a smorgasbord of baits during one trip.

Collecting a season's supply of leeches is easy in the spring when water temperature reaches the magic 50-degree mark and leeches can swim into the traps. The most common leech trap is probably a coffee can in which the sides have been crimped down over some liver or other bait. Punch a hole in the top of the can and attach a small float. (Some anglers use Styrofoam balls; but less-trusting types use small sticks that attract less attention.) Ten- to 12-can traps improve chances of getting enough bait.

A baited gunnysack works well, too. Leeches can squeeze through the loosely woven fabric. Use dead animals found on the

Uni-Knot

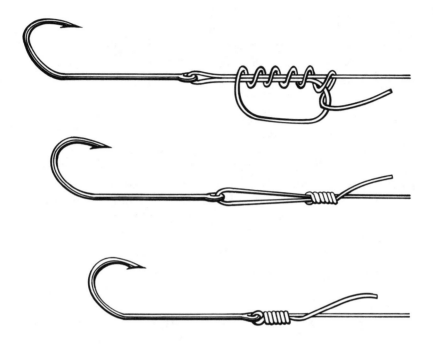

Using a good, secure knot is important in bait fishing, especially when using leeches. The uni-knot is a good, all-purpose knot.

road for bait. It's also possible to get leeches to attach themselves to submerged boards. A board soaked in fish oil and then submerged near the bank overnight can attract a lot of leeches, too.

If using the right container, you can encourage the leeches to sort themselves. For example, horse leeches have strong suckers enabling them to climb the sides of a minnow bucket or Styrofoam box. If you stash your holding box in shallow water overnight, the horse leeches will most likely leave, eliminating the nasty sorting process.

Basic Presentations

Because leeches spend most of their life attached to the bottom of plants or other structure, presentations placing bait in these "normal" areas of habitat clearly work better than open-water, mid-depth presentations. Leeches also work well in river fishing if used with snagless sinker rigs, like the Gapen Bait Walker or the Lindy Rig.

However, hooking leeches can be very difficult. Most leeches will hang onto your hand by the attachment sucker. Some anglers wear a leather or rubber glove, enabling them to slide hooks across their palms. Then they tip the hook up through the leech's sucking mouth.

The leech must be hooked through the strong sucker structure in order for the hook to stay put. Hooking a leech anywhere else simply improves the fishery when the leech flies off during the cast! There will be lots of thrashing and wiggling when you insert the hook, but the hooked leech will return to its normal sidewinder undulation once it is in the water. Boaters might want to carry a cup of dry sand in a shallow tin. Let the sand warm in the sun, then drop the leech from the water on the sand. Wait 15 or 20 seconds and, when the leech stiffens, hook up. As soon as the bait hits the water, its usual wiggle will return.

Rigging Leeches

As always, less is more when baits are active and fish are sulking in warm water. A tiger or small ribbon leech hooked lightly through the head on a light wire No. 8- or 10-hook is an ideal bait for an ultra-light spinning outfit. Trout and smallmouth bass will maul leeches cast to cover in reservoirs, natural lakes and ponds. These leaders can be rigged under bobbers or with a sliding sinker and a floating jig head instead of a bare hook. The floating jighead rig ensures that the leech doesn't latch onto the bottom or hide in a hole. Leeches also work well in combination with in-line or leadhead spinners and spoons. For best results on the retrieve, reel half as fast as you think you should, raising the rodtip a foot or two. Pause. Then follow the leech as it swims toward the bottom. If the leech stops moving, gently raise the rodtip until you feel resistance. It may be a fish. Feel a throb? Set the hook!

Basic Leech Techniques

Although it's possible, and at times productive, to fish leeches in a single spot under a bobber, these wiggling little devils seem ideally suited for slow trolling or cast-and-retrieve action in slow-moving to still waters. Leeches work well with certain trolling

Leech Walking-Sinker Rig

A walking sinker with a leech works well when fishing rocky bottoms. This rig helps prevent the bait from getting lost in the rocks. A spinner blade can be used to provide a little flash.

methods in rivers. They seem particularly productive in marshy areas, as well as at the mouths of bog-fed streams.

Moving Water. Where the bottom is very uneven, boat and bank anglers can reduce the number of snags and the amount of lost terminal tackle by using bottom-bouncer rigs. Some rigs have a wire stem holding the sinker off bottom and over the snags; others, like Gapen's Bait Walker, a mini-spreader, bounce the bait over hazards. With most of these, all you add to enjoy action is a 2- to 3-foot-long leader, a No. 4 or 6 hook and one or more leeches.

On even bottoms, bobbers give you greater control over bait placement. A translucent casting float rigged 4 feet above a lightly hooked leech and shotted just enough so the bait occasionally ticks bottom remains the shallow-water choice where longer casts

Slip-Sinker Rig For Leeches

A leech on a slip-sinker rig works particularly well for walleyes. In this case, the leech is hooked on a floating jig. This keeps the leech out of the weeds.

are needed. In shallow or fairly slow water, wire-stem bobbers cock nicely without adding weight to the unweighted leech. In deeper water, a rig with split shot off the end of the line and a leech hooked to a dropper loop a foot or so off the bottom makes the presentation more visible and eliminates most rig losses.

Still Water. Presenting leeches just off the bottom or along the edge of weedbeds can be done several different ways. High-tech fishermen slowly backtroll an unweighted leech off a downrigger ball. This is done both with or without spinners or cowbell trolling gangs. Backtrolling permits the use of heavier lines than can be cast; this can be very useful when challenging big fish and tackle-eating snags.

Backtrolling leeches rigged on slip-sinker outfits is a favorite method for taking walleyes in rivers. It's also effective in still water. When backtrolling, remember to fish at slow speeds. Canoe trollers do this by trailing a sinking fly line in order to reach even summer-deep walleyes.

Canoe trollers, and those who row prams or skiffs, enjoy considerable advantages while trolling leeches and other baits. The "fast/slow" boat and bait speed and depth variation seems more attractive to most fish than a set, unchanging motorized speed. If rowing, you're facing toward your trolled bait. This gives you a better view of your rod's action as the leech does its thing.

Modest-sized bobber rigs work well when fished just off weedbeds or in sand, gravel or rocky bottom areas without stick-ups, weeds and other snags; however, an unweighted leech hooked through the head with a double-weight hook does the job on 2- to 6-pound-test line. Short casts require careful approaches, and, as always with unweighted baits, you must follow the bait with your rodtip. If the bait pauses, line twitches occur at the surface or the leech suddenly changes directions, pick up the slack. If you feel weight, set the hook. Use only a shot or two of weight, if necessary.

7

Presenting The Worm And Leech

V eteran outdoor writer Ed Park once wryly noted, "You should only plan fishing trips after you hear the fishing is awful, because it's sure to change before you get there." Clearly, anyone can catch fish—even with crude methods and unsuitable baits—when conditions are right. The proof of this certainly must be worms, America's most popular live bait.

Fish simply don't "see" very many worms in natural settings; therefore, some experts feel worms are overrated as bait when compared with crayfish, minnows or even insects. These same experts hold that leeches are both underrepresented and underrated. So why do so many anglers fish with worms? Simple, these baits are easy to obtain and maintain. Because just about everyone uses them, they will naturally take more fish. They also are well-suited for muddy water conditions when fish are expecting a bonus meal, and they are a convenient backup bait for desperate anglers.

Bank And Boat

Boaters and shore anglers normally face different problems that have different solutions.

Even though boaters can use some of the rigs and methods designed for bank anglers, they usually do better with systems that take advantage of a boat's increased mobility and access. Boaters' systems divide into four types: anchoring or trolling in either moving or still water. Each approach requires different rigs and differ-

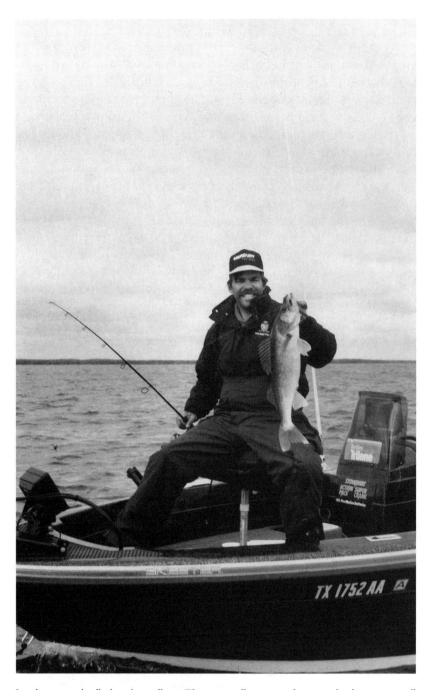

Leeches are a deadly bait for walleye. This nice walleye was taken on a leech cast into still water.

Presenting The Worm And Leech　　　　　　　　　　87

ent ways of using leeches and worms as bait.

Anchoring or keeping the boat stationary offers the opportunity for maximum concentration on a specific—usually small—area that you hope holds fish. This approach is good for covering key structure, such as weedbed coves, submerged stream channels and other known spots where either the fishfinder shows fish or fish have been found in the past. Using a hunting analogy, it's a rifle rather than a shotgun approach! A pair of small anchors that can be noiselessly inserted into the water are less disturbing to the fish and the bottom. (Remember to shut off your motor and let the boat glide quietly into position.)

One of the best leech-fishing methods for stationary boat anglers is called "shaking." Hooking fish this way is easy, but landing fish that are hooked in submerged "shrubbery" may require practice and judicious pruning. The rig is simple: a terminal hook of your choice and a small split shot lightly squeezed onto 8- or 10-pound-test line for panfish, and heavier line if you expect bass.

This system seems to work best in the least accessible, overgrown areas on most lakes and ponds; therefore, the boat needs to be eased far back onto cover, such as submerged treetops. After the leech is lowered through the shrubbery, carefully shake the branches that are sticking up out of the water or push on submerged branches with a long pole. This apparently stirs up fish on those dead days when nothing much is happening. Panfish, bass and other species soon become active. If you don't get a fish in a short time in this tight structure, try another spot. If the water is stained or the structure is near a stream or mud bank, try worms as well for variety.

Sideplaners will place the bait near the bank without spooking fish when you are fishing from a moving boat. They also increase the amount of water you can cover. With paired sideplaners, the deep-water planer usually tows a minnow.

The keys are the "dropback" distance from planer to bait and the rig's running depth. Any speed works so long as it's slow! The dropback distance should be minimal—10 to 15 feet at most. Longer dropbacks are more difficult to control when you vary planer direction in order to cover irregular shoreline; the baits hang up on the points, too. A Bait Walker or spreader-type sinker combined with a trailing leader to the rigged bait keeps weeds from running down the line to the bait. A three-way-swivel setup with

Tandem Hook Rig

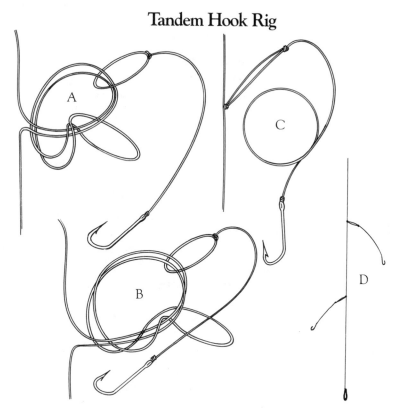

Here is a quick way to tie a tandem hook rig when you're fishing leeches or minnows or both. In "A" the main line is looped through the loop on the leadered hook; then the hook is brought through the line's loop (B). Then repeat the process for a second dropper.

a dropper loop (which is half the test of the main line) going to a sinker works, too. Both methods let the trolled worm or leech run near but not on the bottom. Depth can be adjusted by varying boat speed and dropback length.

Worm and leech rigs for trolling depend upon the fish species sought. As a rule, worms troll best when either threaded onto special rigs or used in multiple-hook harnesses. Worms also troll reasonably well at slow speeds when rigged on plastic-worm hooks with a barb near the hook's eye holding the worm's head in place. If nightcrawlers are used, a second, smaller hook on a short leader can be hooked near the worm's tail to pick up nibblers.

A wire panfish rig or two No. 8 snelled hooks rigged 2 feet apart and a foot above a dipsey sinker make a standard bottom-fishing setup. Put a nice worm on one hook and a leech on the other. Fished from a boat, canoe or even a float tube, the result is double treats drifting. This works well from a zippy bass boat with an electric motor and a state-of-the-art fishfinder. It also works from a paddled canoe or from a carefully positioned boat that drifts in the wind along the outside edge of weedbeds. (Experience suggests that a smaller craft, such as a canoe or inflatable johnboat, may be the easiest to control.) Lift the bait and it will usually move faster than the boat for a short time. This is the time when fish often hit a leech; worms seem to draw more strikes when they're not moving.

The sinker-to-lower-hook distance can make a big difference when fishing in underwater weeds of approximately the same height and depth with fish holding just under the weed tops. By moving the first hook farther from the sinker, the worm or leech will be on top of the weeds making a better presentation. At the same time, this will reduce the time spent cleaning weeds off the hook. When weeds of the same height are growing on a bottom that is irregular and depth changes rapidly, a bobber rig is sometimes the better choice.

Narrow weedbeds, such as those often found in steep shoreline areas, necessitate a long rod that can reach over the weeds and put the bait on the inside breakline. Some good fish can be found in these spots because they are protected both from boaters who cast along the outside of the weedbeds and from shore anglers who normally will announce their presence before getting set up to fish. This is why British and European bank anglers set up on legless seats behind bushes and other cover, wear dull clothing and stay put. This improves their chances of taking shore-cruising fish that usually hug the bank.

If you can keep your boat from blowing in too close to shore, try fishing the downwind shore of the lake. Again, fish the inside break if the weeds do not stick out of the water far enough to trap floating baits; otherwise, fish the outside edge. Then slowly troll into the wind trailing a minnow, leech or worm. Change rigs and drift down along the shore. This is a prime method to use after major storms occur on large waters, because enough surf is kicked up to kill bait of all types. Cruise the shore the morning after a storm and load the boat! (Double drifting also works with other combinations: Leech and minnow, salamander and minnow, and worm and minnow combos are certainly worth a try.)

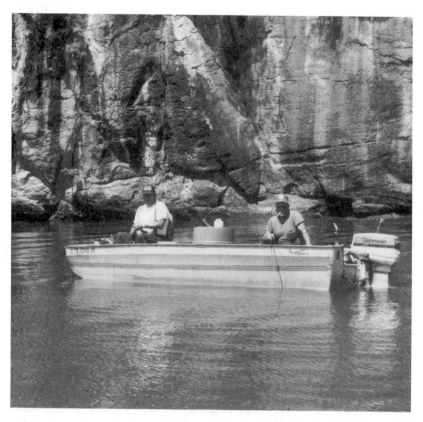

Simply floating downstream while dragging a worm can mean success for boat fishermen. These anglers are prepared to make an effective presentation.

Few river shoreline methods beat floating downstream in a small boat with a couple of baits over the stern and a good hand on the tiller. Worms and leeches are perfect for this system. Riggings vary wildly according to water depth, speed and clarity and bottom type.

Unweighted baits don't work well in this situation because their position and depth cannot be controlled. Sinkers serve the angler best in moderate to fast water, but the distance from sinker to bait is critical. The longer the distance, the more latitude in depth the bait enjoys. If you need the bait to hug bottom, you need to shorten the leader. So-called bottom-walking sinkers help avoid snags; the bait passes over them. Some anglers rig droplines with terminal shot so the weights will snag and pull off, saving the hook and bait.

Where water is running too fast or too deep for split shot, anglers use surgical tubing holders attached to a swivel rig. Sometimes, they use short sections of the tubing, slit and strung on the line. Pieces of lead wire are inserted in the tubing as sinker weight.

Species like trout or striped bass that cruise lakes searching for chow are prime candidates for bank-bound anglers who can stay put in prime spots near inlets and outlets or fish points and narrows where fish concentrate. Productive systems with worms and leeches include bobber and bottom rigs.

"Injecting" the worms with air gives the bottom-rigged bait enough buoyancy to be especially attractive to trout and stripers. Add just enough air to the worm's tail end to bring the worm and its hook up off bottom. You can check the amount by dunking the hooked worm in water.

Rigs That Move Worms

Among the best methods for moving worms are the well-known Texas and Carolina plastic-worm rigs. In each case, the line runs through an egg or the bullet-shaped sinker. If the water is murky, try the brass worm sinkers for a bit of extra flash.

Texas rigging involves tying the line directly to the hook after running the line through a worm sinker, then threading a worm on the hook to a point about midway between the worm's head and collar. The hook is turned so the point can be buried in the worm near the collar, making it weedless. It's also possible to use a hook with a weed guard or even a floating jig-head hook. When a fish picks up the worm, it feels no resistance because the line can run free, and the rig rarely hangs up because of the weedless threading. The worm will last longer if you add a tiny split shot ⅛ inch ahead of the hook and pull the worm up over the hook's eye and knot. This rig works best with the smallest possible weight on a fairly clear bottom. Long-shank No. 10 hooks work well with red worms; bigger hooks are used with nightcrawlers.

The Carolina rig varies from the Texas rig: The worm sinker is fixed on the line a short distance above the hook. On the worm-and-swivel rig, a small bead is placed between the weight and the knot that connects the line to the barrel swivel; the bead protects the knot. A variable-length leader requires a hook size that matches your worm—No. 4, No. 2 or 1/0 usually are used with big nightcrawlers.

A basic crawler rig was all that was necessary to tempt this green sunfish into biting. The key is making sure the worm looks natural on the hook; it shouldn't ball up.

If the worm is not sufficiently buoyant, it should be air-injected or fished off a floating jig head. Then, while the weight drags and bounces on the bottom, the worm rides over the top of weeds and structure avoiding snagging. Leader length, of course, varies with the depth and thickness of bottom cover. Such a rig, like the stationary floating worm or Biggie bobber rig, lets you fish a set distance off the bottom.

During the summer doldrums, it's not unusual to feel the nips and nibbles of small panfish, but some are really lazy lunkers. Adding a short leader to the front hook eye and inserting a No. 8 light wire hook in the worm's tail will nab those nibblers. You can also attach an open-eye No. 10 Siwash to the bend of your main hook. Open-eye singles are also handy for replacing the trebles on lures in order to change hang-ups to hookups.

Bank Fishing On Moving Water

Fishing from stream banks can be extremely productive; however, anglers must be willing to walk for one to two hours to increase their distance from the parking lot before starting to fish. This technique puts you a satisfactory distance from those who fish from their cars, and it lets you fish while making your way back toward your transportation.

Usually, meandering streams will have a deep, outer bank—the side to fish with worms or leeches! Rig a leech or worm on a terminal hook and add a small shot. Try to get within half of a fishing rod's length of the water and submerge the rodtip until it's 6 inches off the bottom. Then, slowly let out line. This should drop your bait into downstream pockets where the large fish lurk. This method works up to 50 or so feet downstream. If you are farther than that, your line will hang up. Work each "cast" at least five minutes, stopping your bait in prime spots off rocks and stumps for up to a minute or two per stop. It takes time to tempt a wallhanger!

Big fish tend to go after big baits. Even in a trout stream, a lusty leech or 9-inch worm can lure a big brown or bass.

Although this system works well in moderate currents, it doesn't do well in slow flows; however, add a bobber and you're still in business! Two different rigs, both with the same basics, will work.

The bobber floats your bait to the fish at the speed of the current. This seems more productive when worms are used over an even bottom so the bait can work just off the bottom. This also works when fishing grasshoppers in meadow streams.

When the bottom is uneven and fish aren't rising, a system the British call "stet pegging" works best. It's the same bobber with split shot nipped to the end of the line. The bait is fished off a foot-long dropper tied 18 inches above line's end. The bobber-to-split-shot distance is more than the stream depth, so you need enough shot to just barely sink the bobber. This rig provides intensive coverage similar to the sunken rodtip system with considerably greater downstream range.

Cast the bobber or let it drift downstream on a tight line. When the split shot touches bottom, it will stop. Reel line in until it is moderately taut. Raising the rodtip and bobber should pull the shot off bottom. Drop the rodtip again and the shot should settle back on the bottom just a few inches downstream. In moderate stream flows, this system offers solid coverage for up to 50 yards. No other method works so well on lockjawed steelhead and salmon!

Each of these systems offers lateral coverage that, for bank fishing, is limited to only a single rod length. Those who wade would be able to double that coverage. This is reason enough for using a long rod. When stet pegging, for example, you can move the rodtip sideways to shift the bobber so the bait moves 6 inches or so laterally. As a rule, it works best to extend the rod fully at a right angle to the current, establishing the greatest lateral depth. Then each time you cast, point the rodtip downstream until it's almost parallel with the bank. The big advantage of this system is coverage intensity. If fish are in a given run, you can just about tap them on the nose with your bait, and your bait is in the water—not being retrieved or cast.

Baitfish Basics

8

Minnows

innows confuse even taxonomists. With over 230 species in North America, species identification boggles the mind. No other bait comes in so many flavors, considering the variations in size, coloration and species. Minnows are, by definition, fish having one dorsal fin, abdominal pelvic fins, a lateral line, no teeth and a scaled body.

Their diets vary wildly, too. Some minnows feed on crustaceans and insects; others eat algae. Some are mid-water types; others lurk near the bottom. Some, like carp, are quite large. Some, like dace, are very small. Some, like goldfish, are introduced; some, like Mad toms, are native, although they can be found far from their native climes. Along with baitfish, minnows are the best available live bait for large gamefish.

The reason for this is simple. Given the choice, fish always will try to eat the biggest and easiest-to-capture food they can find. Small fish, like fingerling trout, start out eating insects; however, when they reach a foot or so in length, they become minnow munchers. Clearly, anglers in search of wallhangers won't do better than minnows and baitfish, providing, of course, minnows are the right species, type and size to suit the quarry's palate.

Minnow Behavior

Most minnows are, by nature, shoal fish that move in unison when in fast water or when threatened by a predator. When they

If minnows are balled up in the tank's corners and are fighting to get out of the dip net, you are most likely buying bait that is in reasonably good condition. If they're listless and swim near the top, don't take them.

Minnows

are feeding, minnows move in rather loose groups. These groups can tighten quickly into a compact mass of similar-sized fish separated by just less than a body length with a 45-degree offset to the side or top. This configuration helps fish inside the shoal swim with less effort and, when the shoal is threatened, individuals can scatter in all directions, confusing predatory fish.

Special cells—the lateral-line neuromas that, in baitfish, have outside contact through a series of pores—let minnows sense their position within the school. Predatory species, such as pike, carry the same neuromas on the skin surface for maximum reception. If minnows were built this way, they could easily expire from sensory overload!

The minnow's characteristic quick movements confuse predators. However, as soon as an individual minnow's action slows or changes noticeably from that of the group, it's marked as easy prey. Hook a minnow in the right place—through the nose, small of the tail, under the chin latch or under the dorsal fin—and it might as well carry a sign that says, "Eat me." This is true even when it's presented in a shoal of free-swimming minnows. Thus, the unnatural becomes the "natural" in presenting your bait.

In some cases, it may take some doctoring. When fishing big minnows on light wire hooks, for example, you can remove a fin or two to achieve that "easy prey" look. Judicious fin-clipping, like proper hook location, keys the type of baitfish action you're seeking.

For example, if both pectoral fins are removed, baitfish tend to dive. This trimming, like an extra heavy hook impaled under the fish's chin latch, can cause the bait to move down into the action without additional shots that might hang up in the weeds. With one pectoral fin removed, the minnow swims in circles. If the bait is so frisky that it pulls your bobber under, and you don't use a bigger, less sensitive bobber, simply snip off half of the bait's tail to slow down its progress.

A fish with all fins removed will roll upside down because its center of gravity is above its swim bladder. That's why dead or dying fish will roll belly-up. This kind of "dynamic stability" affords the fish maximum maneuverability in catching its dinner.

Minnow Shapes And Sizes
The minnow's shape also affects its effectiveness as bait. All

Complete Angler's Library

Comparing the size and shape of the shiner (top) and the dace shows why the dace would be a better choice for small-mouthed gamefish. For a more natural look, hook the minnow either through the lips or under the dorsal fin.

minnows, except perhaps goldfish, have a rather long, thin body that will slide down a gamefish's throat nicely. This assumes, of course, the bait will fit in the target species' mouth. Nobody is successful in trying to take crappies with 5-inch minnows, whatever the bait's shape!

Minnow size varies by species, and all species will grow during the year. Size is more important than species among minnows and other schooling baitfish. Within a given species, individual size tends to be very uniform. After the hatch, minnows in schools will be the same, small size; however, they will grow over the summer to prepare for the next fall or spring spawning. Matching the size and, where possible, the natural-bait species in the water you're fishing makes sense even though some gamefish aren't always that fussy.

Tests with schooling striped bass, however, showed a 50 percent decline in the catch rate for each 1-inch length difference in size between the bait and the native bait of the waters being fished. This is most important where the fish are working natural-bait schools and, therefore, have more numerous dinner selections available to them.

Visibility also is a factor in the choice of baitfish. Some minnows, like silver shiners, come equipped with considerable flash that makes them more visible to gamefish. Others, such as chubs, promote a dull appearance. Given the choice, silver and other bright reflective baits are excellent for use in off-colored waters. Fish do see colors differently from humans, and the visual acuity of individual gamefish species varies, as well. Because freshwater fish habitat runs toward blues and greens, fish see reds best. That's why red appears as a spawning color in a number of species and why baitfish with red fins and other red markings work so well. (A slash of red lipstick along either side of your bait should improve results.)

Some rather subtle variations occur within species which may make a big difference in your success ratio, too. For example, many West Coast live-bait anglers claim that blue-backed anchovies produce more and bigger striped bass in brackish bays than the more common "green-backs."

Baitfish colors also vary during the year and, in some species, between males and females. Generally, males will remain the most colorful during the year, reaching peak colors during the spring or fall spawning periods. The brighter males often seem to be the choice bait. However, some walleye fishermen have found that female fatheads attract more fish. Perhaps predators have found that pregnant female fatheads offer more calories per gram.

In situations where water is deeply off-color and gamefish are forced to hunt more by taste or hearing, oily baitfish, such as alewives, shad or smelt, appear to work best. This can also be a good time for using a combination bait of a live minnow and an oily dead bait, such as salt herring. Fish oil and other similar attractants seem to offer the greatest improvement in results under these conditions.

Habitat And Distribution
Minnow habitat varies widely, too, from clear headwater streams

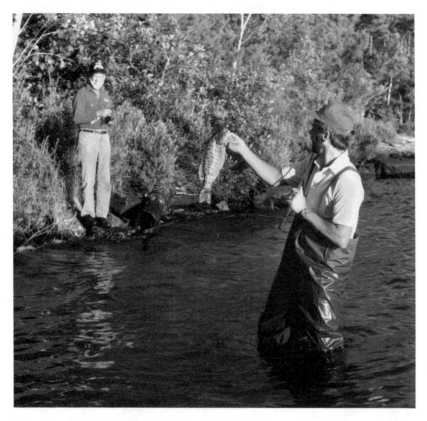

Once these anglers knew what the smallmouths were feeding on, they simply "matched the hatch." This brought them some great smallies.

to muddy marshes. Even though just about any minnow species will catch fish, matching your bait with resident minnows will help you take advantage of the "injured straggler" syndrome in minnow shoals that's so alluring to hungry gamefish. For whatever reasons, minnows native to moving water produce best in moving water; minnows from still water better suit still-water fishing. This "match the hatch" approach doesn't always matter, except on "lockjaw" days. It's helpful to know which species you're dealing with and its preferred habitat. This, then, starts with minnow identification.

Identification And Selection

Serious anglers who buy, as well as catch, their bait need to be able to identify the minnows they use. Bait sellers don't always sell

These crappies fell victim to enticing live-minnow offerings. Pick minnows that inhabit the same temperature zone as that of the crappies.

what they claim—chubs and shiner species, for example, are easily confused. Some species are more durable while others are more attractive; few offer both characteristics. Second, gamefish will look for minnows where they are present naturally. Therefore, it's also important to know the minnow's temperature and habitat preferences. Having knowledge of the particular species' behavior is obviously beneficial. Knowing the temperature preferences of the gamefish you're seeking and of various minnows helps you match the right bait and quarry. There are several freshwater fish field guides that can help you make the best choice if you feel you need more information than is provided here.

The chart that appears in Chapter 10 includes pertinent information on most of the common minnow species. Some are sold under regional aliases: Fatheads, for example, are also known as mud minnows. A great many less common or regional species also take fish, however. If water-temperature preferences for these species are not known, check the temperature of the water in which you find them. Then check the preferred temperature of the gamefish you're seeking. Where there is a match, you can usually catch fish.

Some local and regional bait preferences often seem largely accidental. In fact, many depend more on what bait dealers are able to keep easily than on the bait itself. Sometimes it is a matter of someone taking a big fish on a certain minnow—which may have been an accident—and others switching to the same bait.

A few general rules help. Broadly speaking, chubs offer superb hardiness and sufficient size to tempt pike and other large gamefish. Dace work better for trout and smaller stream species. Fatheads, the most durable minnows, are popular because they are easy to raise. Goldfish are tough—and cheap—but should not be used in waters where they are not already present.

Shiners, which are fragile and, if large, an awkward shape for gamefish to swallow, make excellent bait for largemouth bass, pike and other predatory species that prowl near shore. Golden shiners seem a rather sturdy substitute for emerald shiners at many bait shops, partly because they tolerate warmer water. Other spe-

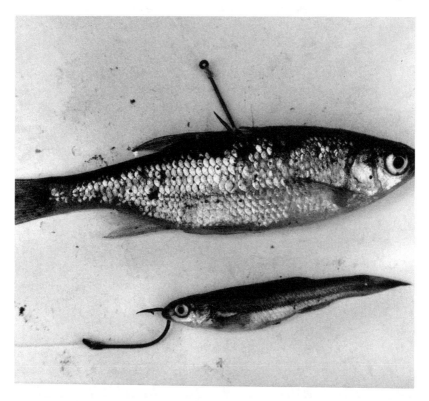

Comparing a shiner (top) and a dace reveals reasons why these baits would be more effective with different-sized gamefish. The streamlined dace is better for trout and small gamefish while the fragile shiner's shape is more acceptable for gamefish with large mouths.

cies differ in preferred temperatures, habitat and other factors that anglers should carefully consider.

Care And Feeding Of Minnows

Anyone who has ever kept fish knows that bait is difficult to preserve. Savvy bait dealers keep minnows and baitfish in cool, aerated water. Ideally, baitfish should be lively and bright-looking. They should not have damaged skin, red noses from bumping into tanks or missing scales from too much handling. Good bait "balls up" in a tank corner near the bottom; bad bait skitters about near the surface or just bellies-up. Good bait wiggles wildly while being transferred from tank to net; bad bait just flops. Don't pay for hardy baitfish and then take a fragile substitute! Insist on an oxygenated bag, if available.

Most fishermen who complain about poor quality of today's minnows create more problems with poor care, over-crowded containers, high temperatures or lack of oxygen.

Minnows do best if they're not crowded. Figuring on a fish-per-gallon basis, 18 small minnows or six large ones are the limit. Separate cylindrical gallon containers work well for small batches of minnows. This encourages you to try more than one type, and cylindrical containers help head off "corner pileup" and the resulting injuries that damage minnows in rectangular tanks. Old water jugs also make excellent minnow buckets.

Place the bait buckets in a large container, such as a big cooler. The cooler keeps the buckets from rolling about or upsetting. Add some ice and it will keep your minnow bucket's water temperature between 50 and 65 degrees. Remove any dead or dying minnows and save them in a sealable plastic bag on ice for use as cut bait or chum. An alternative would be to place bags of ice or, even better, frozen cartons of water in your minnow container to keep things cool.

Oxygen is also a necessary ingredient. Some bait shops offer bait bagged in water from their own oxygenated tank. The sealed bag is then placed in a box and, if kept cool, should keep minnows in good shape for a couple of days. (This is, after all, the way tropical fish are shipped from Brazil to Florida and other U.S. destinations.) As water temperature rises, water loses its ability to hold oxygen and crowding becomes a critical factor. Battery-powered aerators work off car, boat or flashlight batteries; 110-volt aquarium aerators will handle large bait-stock tanks at home. Stop-gap methods include using oxygen tablets that create bubbles, stirring water with an egg beater or removing water and shaking it up in a barrel. And then there is the method applied by a Kansas teenager: a funnel and rubber hose. Clamped to the car window, the funnel faces forward with the hose leading to the bait container. The faster the teenager drove, the more oxygen bubbles there were in the water.

Trolling buckets and other drag-along containers work very well for boaters when surface waters are cool; however, they are poor choices when surface temperatures rise in summer. These buckets can't be left in the water when the boat is traveling at high speeds, either. Shore anglers who put their minnow buckets in a lake or stream find that their minnows turn fins-up. They should move them to a spot where current, or wave action, will help ensure more adequate oxygenation. Sinking a minnow bucket to deeper, cooler water can improve survival rates, too.

Live shiners can take gamefish when all else fails. However, keeping shiners and other delicate species from doing the backstroke without an aerator can be a problem. Aerators do quit for one reason or another. It's best to have a backup or alternative system if the aerator fails.

Catching Your Own Bait

Serious live-bait anglers can catch their own minnows for bait in various ways. You can make it a sporting event, like in England, by using the lightest tackle available, tiny hooks and minibaits. A light weight fly outfit, 5-foot ultra-light spinning gear with 2-pound-test line or even a simple cane pole will work.

Another method is practiced by cast netters who spin and fling their circular nets ringed with weights so that the edges drop faster than the center. The net engulfs the bait before the caster hauls it in by the rope attached to the net's center. The technique looks wonderfully smooth and easy, but it takes practice. You hold a lead or, if you're smart, a cork "tooth saver" in your teeth and the edge of the net in each hand. Then you spin with the grace of a ballerina and release and toss a perfect circle that can engulf more baitfish than a parcel of pelicans could consume. That's the theory. There is, however, a certain fascination to cast netting: flinging a perfectly circular net that offers a reward even if it doesn't

When you have mastered the art of cast-net throwing, the net should open fully like this. Casters often use bread or cracker crumbs to attract baitfish.

catch any bait. With experience, one learns to spot subtle signs indicating the presence of baitfish, relying then on target casting rather than chance casting.

Dip nets, either the umbrella frame or the handled landing-net style, don't require the practice needed for using either cast nets or seines. Special dip nets can be found in most fishing catalogs. Umbrella nets work best from piers or boats in waters without snags; dip nets work better in streams or shallows. A few crackers or other chum, such as finely crushed egg shells, can bring minnows over submerged nets. It's also possible to attract minnows over nets. Dragging a spoon tipped with a pork rind over the top also works. Frugal anglers have even made fine-mesh inserts for their favorite landing net.

Seines are especially suited for shoreline bait-gathering in areas relatively free of snags, weeds or other hindrances, such as snakes or 'gators. These long rectangular nets have weights on the bottom and floats on the top. If you stir up the mud a bit, you will stir up food. This attracts minnows that don't see your net because of the muddy water. Seining does require at least two people. While one seiner stays in place, the other wades along the shore in water about as deep as the net's height. When the net is fully extended, both seiners can start moving toward the shore. Then

Complete Angler's Library

the bottom of the net is swept up so the bait is gathered in the bag. Nets that are 20 or 30 feet long and 4 feet high seem big enough for most anglers. Mesh sizes can vary according to the size of your quarry. Nets will last longer if they are soaked in a bucket of linseed oil each spring. Nets should be stored in newspaper to keep the mesh dry and reduce rot. Anglers should repair the mesh and replace missing leads and floats at the end of the season rather than in the spring when the minnows are running.

Commercial, conical, wire-mesh traps baited with some stale bread work well when either suspended beneath buoys in lakes or anchored with rocks to the bottom of streams. Glass traps do the job, too, as do homemade, wire mesh traps. A gallon glass jar with a mesh cone in its mouth makes a good trap. A child-sized life ring or inflatable tube added to one end of a trap makes a nice minnow holder for the bank or pier.

In streams, setting traps above minnow schools which are easy to spot in shoal water works well if you bait the traps and chum with crackers. You need to dump the trap as it fills with fish or the minnows will leave. Wire traps with more durable baits, such as canned cat food in a mesh bag, can be left overnight. A cheap but effective bait is canned corn that's softened a day or two in water. Add oil from anchovies or sardines for an even better bait.

If fishing in lakes, buoyed traps should be set where they won't be snagged by other fishermen. Consider using flotsam and other inconspicuous markers, such as wooden sticks, instead of commercial floats to avoid attracting attention from those that would empty the traps. The traps should be marked with your name and telephone number.

Many states have specific net and trap regulations. Read the regulations before netting or trapping.

9

Other Baitfish

Classed loosely as "other baitfish" if they swim and aren't minnows, these fish are a wildly assorted grab bag of species, each of which will catch something, somewhere, sometime! Numerous baitfish species abound, and anglers who are savvy enough to net or trap their own supply often score better with local species than they do with commercially available baitfish, such as chubs. However, in areas where "gamefish are prohibited as bait," you cannot use yellow perch, crappies or sunfish.

While most minnows school, some baitfish are solitary either by inclination or because of habitat. For example, bottom-dwelling species, such as Mad toms or sculpins, seem quite happy hiding alone under rocks.

The major schooling baitfish species—gizzard shad, alewives, rainbow smelt and even yellow perch—behave much like minnows. The tips in Chapter 8 on catching and keeping minnows would apply to these fish, as well. (Any special ways to catch baitfish will be covered in this chapter.) Most larger baitfish can be taken on ultra-light tackle utilizing very small hooks and grubs.

Suckers And Chubs

Believers in the logical theory "big fish take big baits" know why suckers or golden shiners up to a foot long are so popular in the South. They're fished under balloons as a bait for giant bass. Most put a 1/0 or 2/0 hook through the body, just above the anal

The alewife (top), gizzard shad (second from top), killifish and white sucker (bottom) are among the most popular species of baitfish. The oiliness of the alewife and shad make them particularly attractive to gamefish.

Other Baitfish

fin. When it's hot and the big bass are deep, these anglers hook them like they would minnows—in the throat latch or lip—and either remove the pectoral fins or add a sinker to take the bait down. Northern anglers can use the same rigs for muskies or pike.

Because there are 63 sucker species, these rather ugly bottom-feeders are so numerous that they are the largest biomass in many streams and lakes. There should be no problem in finding these durable baits. Because they overwinter well, suckers also are a good choice for ice fishermen—fishing them under tip-ups for pike is a popular pastime in the Midwest.

Mad Toms

Mad toms, an undersized species of bullhead (catfish), offer the catfish virtues of availability and durability. Most specimens run under 5 inches in length and hang out in rocky, sandy or gravelly runs in smaller streams. (It's easy to see why they are favorite smallmouth and trout baits.) Some species are most common near vegetation.

Catching Mad toms couldn't be easier; they are always baits of opportunity. When you run out, simply bash a rock on a submerged rock, roll it over and collect the stunned bait. Replace the submerged rock carefully so it will form a nice, shaded hidey-hole again. Carry a mini-net, like those used in tropical fish stores. These nets also help catch hellgrammites, crayfish and other elusive baits.

Because Mad toms like to hide under and in things, they can be caught in pop-top cans strung together in a batch and submerged in rocky habitat overnight. Don't worry about keeping these sturdy little fish; Mad toms will survive for a season when kept in submerged cages or aerated tanks. Fishing Mad toms on bottom rigs for trout, walleye and smallmouths in rocky rivers and larger streams offers superb results.

Sculpins, Also Known As Muddlers

Sculpin family members, like the various Mad toms, prefer clear water that's cold and fast-moving. Such water delivers dinner to a fish that, because of its pectoral fin spines, its resemblance to an airplane wing cross section and, most of all, its lack of swim bladder, sticks tight to bottom.

Most of the 300 species of sculpins are marine. Several, like

A pet store is a good place to look for a container to carry the sculpins you have collected. Sculpins, or muddlers as they are sometimes called, are easy to catch.

the California bullhead, are important brackish water baits for striped bass and other estuarine gamefish. Identifying individual species is difficult even for experts; however, some general rules apply. For example, species from small, cold streams appear to have fewer prickles and spines than those from warmer water and slow to still waters. Mottled sculpins, sometimes called bullheads and sometimes called "muddlers" (alluding either to their tendency to simply muddle about or to their fly imitation), are favored by trout and other stream species both east and west.

Muddlers aren't any more difficult to catch than Mad toms. The same techniques apply. A net held downstream while rocks are turned over reduces the need for desperation grabs. Sculpins, like minnows, do nicely in aquariums or bait barrels, eating goldfish food and just about anything else. Exceptionally durable on the hook, they are a wonderful bait when fished on or near bottom in moderate- to fast-moving water. (Spiny marine species in brackish water and freshwater species taken from slow water produce more bites if their spines are trimmed; they roll in the current. Otherwise, they use their spines to jam in and hide under rocks.)

Along with crayfish, Mad toms and minnows, sculpins seem to be the best baits available for big brown trout and river smallmouths. These gamefish pick sculpins up rather gingerly. There will be a bite, a long pause as the gamefish bites down and some easy movement as the sculpin is turned and swallowed head-first. If you plan to set the hook early—especially for pike and other toothy fish—try a special double-needle sculpin hook that's inserted through the bait's vent and clipped at the mouth. By using the bait needles, you can insert a leader and add a double hook through the scuplin's vent. Avoid treble hooks if possible; they hang up too often when you fish sculpins off bottom.

Darters

These dandy baits are more closely related to perch than the minnows they resemble. A huge number of species share varied habitats on the bottom of streams or lakes in waters east of the Rocky Mountains. An astonishing variety of colors existing in the rainbow and redband darter males makes species identification interesting for the compulsive fisherman who is not happy with general descriptions. However, most darters work most places most of the time.

All darters seem fairly hearty on the hook, but they don't do well if kept in the typically congested live minnow bucket. Some holdover success results from the use of 50-gallon and larger aquariums; however, darters work best if used right after they're caught.

These species are a good source of unusual baits for savvy fishermen who catch darters by using very small hooks and stump grubs, worm sections or wasp larvae as baits. Because they don't keep well and are rather small, they aren't popular bait-shop fare. They work particularly well on bass, pike and other gamefish in very clear water and after dark. Their generally dark color offers a strong silhouette, and vibrations from their "darting" motion (giving them their name) seem to attract hungry nocturnal predators from long distances. They are an absolutely killer bait for

Complete Angler's Library

Deep-dwelling lake trout found in the Great Lakes are fond of shad, as well as rainbow smelt and alewives. This is because of their oils.

brown trout or arm-long rainbows after dark. Most species also work well for smallmouths and are a good alternative on those days when crayfish aren't producing.

Herring, Alewife, Gizzard Shad, Rainbow Smelt
All these schooling species are good baits for big lake trout, bass, striped bass and other large gamefish if slow-trolled or still fished in likely spots. They go down nicely, and their oil offers more calories for the effort. In freshwater where chumming is legal, a grinder on your gunwale will produce a chum slick that, when spread by wind and current, pulls gamefish into easy casting range. After storms that churn alewives and such against rocky breakwaters and banks, anglers should fish along the shore to take advantage of this natural chum.

Offsetting their obvious attractiveness as a bait is a lack of durability and, at times, what appears to be suicidal tendencies in the bait tank. Placing fewer baitfish in large circular tanks helps the survival rate. Because these are school fish, fishing them below bait schools makes sense. A lip-hooked bait will sound below the school where the lunker stripers and salmon lurk. A lively bait with a small hook through the dorsal fin that is tied to 30 feet of 4-pound-test line with a float, like a small balloon, on the other end acts as a "Judas" bait while trying to stay with the school. However, this presentation only works for about 30 minutes on relatively calm water and not at all on windy days so there are often times when this tactic is not worth the effort.

If you need more casting range, consider shot or a twist-on sinker. Big bobbers are highly recommended with such baits. Center-sliders let you cast your dorsal-fin-hooked bait more than once improving its survival rate and, of course, controlling your depth better.

Many species move into the tributary rivers and brooks to spawn in such numbers that it's easy to dip a whole season's supply. An umbrella net is popular around pilings and piers in open water on lakes and in brackish estuaries. These fish also can be taken on very small flies or tiny baits like worm sections. Fishing for gamefish with fresh baits in rivers or in inlets where baitfish mill about before ascending to natal streams can be extremely hot. But, if bait concentrations reach incredible proportions, hookups will be as likely as winning the lottery! When this happens, you should concentrate on bait-catching for later use.

Ciscoes And Whitefish

Reference guides indicate that Great Lakes whitefish are "among the most taxonomically difficult freshwater fishes in America." But ciscoes seem almost as difficult to separate by species. One thing is certain: Smaller ciscoes and whitefish make excellent baits for most open-water gamefish in reservoirs and lakes. The smallest of these baits also works in moving water.

Catching these baitfish is easy because most ciscoes and whitefish can be caught with tiny flies and other baits. Some of the Rocky Mountain and Sierra Nevada whitefish species offer good sport to fly fishermen during the winter—where waters don't freeze.

Smaller gamefish like this yellow perch are popular forage for bigger gamefish. For this reason, these small gamefish are not legal bait.

Gamefish As Bait

Small gamefish, like hatchery trout, immature crappies, rock bass, bluegills and sunfish, would make excellent bait for trophy gamefish if legal. According to California Fish and Game experts, "about a third of all stocked trout in the 7- to 12-inch range are eaten by big trout and bass within a week of stocking."

For that reason, it's illegal to use gamefish for bait in many states. In California, for example, bluegills and trout are illegal baits. Therefore, fishermen troll huge rainbow-trout-finish plugs.

Striped bass suspended in mid-lake during the summer doldrums feast on bluegills, sunfish, yellow perch or even small crappies. Where legal, some anglers fish them as bait and remove the spines to improve hookups. Big pike and trout over 15 inches long will gobble small panfish, too. Again, it is against the law in

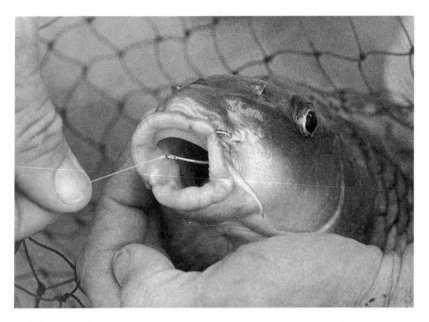

Carp are a good bait, and they are relatively easy to catch. This one went after a single-hook bottom rig baited with a doughball. (The hook is buried to conceal it.)

most states to use any species of gamefish as bait.

Goldfish And The Carp Connection

Small carp—especially goldfish—are durable baits for most gamefish. Striped bass, in particular, seem to be suckers for goldfish. However, neither one should be used as bait unless netted or trapped in the waters you will be fishing.

A number of states prohibit the use of live bait in at least some of their waters. This is to prevent an overpopulation of so-called "rough" fish that can easily destroy a water's natural fishery. Even if legal, concerned anglers will never introduce live minnows or other baitfish in waters where they are not indigenous. It only takes a few goldfish or carp to ruin a fishery. (Goldfish and other carp can live for a long time out of the water so make sure your "dead" baits really are fins-up.)

Eels And Lampreys

Eels (a traditional bait for saltwater fish, such as stripers) and lampreys, which are still a problem in the Great Lakes, can be trolled on harnesses or fished around stream mouths for larger gamefish. Though eels aren't hard to catch on tiny hooks, most are netted or trapped when they run up streams. (Eel chunks work well for catfish.) However, once eels and lampreys are introduced, they are difficult to remove from a fishery.

Uncommon Baitfish

There are several other baitfish species available to anglers who want to catch their own baits. For example, Easterners enjoy using killifish, and there have been some introductions from Europe, such as roach or trench. Southerners have a host of "aquarium species," like Jack Dempseys and various cichlids—tropical spiny-finned freshwater fish—that are quite common in southern Florida.

In the West, native species, such as the tule perch of the San Francisco delta, compete with introduced species, like tilapias (African cichlids.) Lately, as elsewhere in brackish and saltwater areas, species from abroad, like the Japanese loach, have entered American waters via bilge-pumping tankers and steamers. It seems certain that foreign baitfish will continue to make their way into American waters.

=====10=====
Minnow, Baitfish Presentations

Gamefish normally will hit minnows and baitfish near the surface and on the bottom (and sometimes in between) in both still and moving water. The usual bait rigs will work if you've paid attention to the details of bait presentation. A number of those details—such as "matching the hatch," pegging hook size to quarry size and learning more about the bait to be used—already have been mentioned.

Even though systems designed for still water also work in slow-moving current pools and backwaters, there are enough distinctions to require separate treatments for moving and still water. In addition, most waters can be fished from a single spot by wading, bank fishing or casting from an anchored boat, or they are fished "on the fly" by wading or fishing from a moving boat.

Effective Still-Water Systems

Fishing baitfish and minnows in one spot in still water looks simple. Just tie a single hook to the end of some monofilament line, add a minnow and fish. As always, it's the details that make the difference in results because you need to add only the necessary elements to control the baitfish. At least a dozen ways exist for hooking minnows for still-water fishing. Lip hooking is favored when you are casting or trolling the bait. A minnow hooked in front of the dorsal fin forms a horizontal presentation that's ideal for bobber fishing. Tail-hooking is preferred when you want the bait to swim freely.

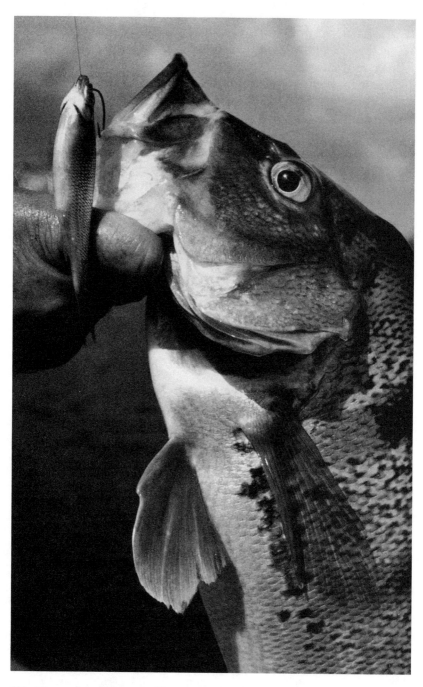

This 4½-pound peacock bass could not resist a basic live-minnow rig pitched to a grass line where the fish waited to ambush unsuspecting forage. Again, "natural presentation" is the key.

Minnow, Baitfish Presentations   121

Because trolling can sometimes mean twisted lines, check along the side of the boat to make sure the bait is tracking properly rather than spinning out of control. An extra long hook inserted through the bait's vent and run out its mouth can make a difference. Special strip-on spinners, long shafts that run through the bait from head to vent with the hook attached to the vent end, work well for this.

Two other setups deserve special mention. In a double minnow setup, the tail of one minnow and the lip of a second are impaled on the same hook in an effort to increase minnow activity. Minnows can be hooked "upside down" on certain floating hooks so their struggle to "right" themselves is an attractant. (Special hooks designed to hold dead baits in the proper position are not recommended for use with live minnows. The minnows' mobility is decreased, and, because the hooks are bulky, their mortality rate increases greatly.)

Freeline And Sinker Presentations

If your minnow is heavy enough to cast, try freelining a minnow that is hooked through the tail. Boaters use this technique around weedbeds and structure and in pocket water. Baits like sculpins that head for the bottom are the choice in Northern waters; in the South, big suckers tempt huge bass. This system also works for pike and muskies. It demands heavy gear, and you must continually pay close attention to your bait's location. To help you keep track of your bait, tie on a small balloon that's inflated to golf ball or softball size—depending on the bait's size and activity. If it becomes jammed in cover, it will pop to free your line.

Sinkers used for stationary still-water rigs aren't, except for the Biggie rig, particularly recommended. Minnows and baitfish get lost in bottom clutter if not hooked with a floating jig head.

Slip-Sinker And Bobber Presentations

Bottom-dwelling gamefish like catfish or lake trout that spend much of their time on or near the bottom are easily taken on slip sinker presentations involving either slow retrieves by shore fishermen or slow backtrolling by boaters. A walking sinker is slid onto line that is tied to a swivel. Two or 3 feet of leader which is 20 percent lower in line test than the main line attaches to the swivel. The baitfish or minnow is lip-hooked on a short-shank

Hooking the minnow or baitfish through the lips works well when the bait is part of a slip-sinker presentation, if the bait is either slowly retrieved or backtrolled.

hook, such as a Siwash, which is about as big across its bend as the depth of the minnow.

A walking or slip sinker is used so when a fish hits the bait, it won't feel any weight on the line and spit out your minnow. In heavily fished areas, the method can radically improve an angler's catch of big browns and largemouths.

Trollers should pull this rig as slowly as possible along drop-offs, the deep-water side of weedbeds and over submerged islands. Fatheads and—if the water's cold enough—emerald shiners work well. If the water's over 70 degrees, however, switch to golden shiners. If the water tops 80 degrees, go for sirens and similar baits.

Casters can use this rig with slow retrieves. Pausing frequently off points or at inlets causes bottom disturbance by the sinker, attracting gamefish from quite a distance.

Medium-sized slip- and fixed-bobber rigs work well with minnows if the bobber is just large enough to prevent the bait from submerging it. In fact, such rigs can tell you when gamefish are approaching the bait as the bobber tips off the minnow's wild gyrations in trying to escape. You can, as noted in a previous chapter, clip some fins to reduce your bait's activity, making it look vulnerable. If the water you fish is less than 6 feet deep or you're trying to tempt fish out from under the edge of weeds or lily pads, use an unweighted minnow and a wire-stem, "self-cocking" bobber for maximum bait movement.

In shallow areas of lakes less than a rod-length deep, try the basic fixed-bobber rig. Hook the minnow just ahead of the dorsal fin or through the lips. Bulk the split shot about 12 inches above the bait so the shot—not the minnow—collects the moss and weeds. For deeper water, switch to a center slider. Over uneven bottom, move to a Biggie or similar rig that will indicate a hit by the "feel." A center-slider bobber without a stop works reasonably well on uneven bottom if there are offshore winds. A small sinker is tied to the end of the line and a dropper keeps the minnow at the distance above bottom where you want to fish. Cast to the spot you've selected and let the sinker drop to the bottom. Tighten the slack until you can feel the sinker; the bobber then will lie at an angle on its side. Hits (which can be felt) will either straighten or submerge the bobber.

Welding Rods For Those Impossible Spots

Welding rods are a big help when you need to penetrate heavy cover. Conventional spinning or, better yet, baitcasting gear that handles 15- to 20-pound-test line will do the job. Common, ordinary welding rods that can be bought at any hardware store will do. Cut them into 10- to 12-inch lengths, pound each end flat and drill a hole in each end. Attach a snap swivel at one end and a snap at the other. Tie the main line to the snap swivel and a No. 4 or 5 light-wire hook, like an Aberdeen, to the other. Light-wire hooks will bend and pull free if snagged. The minnow should be hooked through the lip.

Welding-rod rigs work well in heavy cover where fish hold in summer heat or at midday. Lower the rig in and around submerged tree branches. The stiff-rod leader keeps most fish from winding your line around stumps and branches. If you set the hook in a

A large minnow will attract larger gamefish. This catfish was ready and willing to latch onto the minnow that was freelined into a deep hole. Note the size of the hook used for this catch.

branch, let the line go. The rod's weight usually will pull the hook free. If not, haul back hard and the hook will either bend and pull free or the snap will break. It's easy to add a new snap, hook and bait, but it's also easy to ignore the line abrasion that occurs above the welding rod. Check the line frequently.

Monster Methods In Still And Moving Water

Huge pike, muskies, largemouths and, if you glue a live minnow or baitfish to the bottom, catfish will gobble monster baits up to a foot long. Freelining large shiners into deep holes or under weedbeds can produce huge fish and some incredible collections of vegetation. Big shiners combined with chunks of salt herring on 3/0 hooks produce some monster catfish, too.

Some experts use poke poles and extremely stout line with

these rigs to jerk out big bass and other species from holes in weeds and other heavy cover. Longer rods and poles are an advantage because you can keep a hooked lunker on a short line and reduce the chances of losing the fish because of snags.

Poke Poles And Shaking Minnows

Poke-poling became popular in the West when surf fishermen moved into Clear Lake, California's largest natural lake, and discovered spring bass holed up in extremely thick tules, or bullrushes. Thus, the method got its alternate name, "tule dipping." Poke-poling requires the use of a 12- to 20-foot long fiberglass or cane pole tipped with 18 or 20 inches of cyclone fencing wire, a snap swivel and a No. 2 hook. The rig is baited with a live minnow or frog when used in freshwater; it has an alternative function as a rock and reef outfit in saltwater.

The method is as simple as shoving the rod down into deep weed pockets and under thick floating weed mats in the delta. It also works in thick brush tangles, stumps and other heavy cover which defy the use of usual methods. As subtle as a supersonic bomber, the method produces big fish when and where nothing else works.

Boaters and shore anglers who use long rods or poles find that minnow shaking can be a productive method when all else fails. Gamefish that ambush dinner, such as bass, pike or muskies, often lurk in submerged or partly submerged treetops or brush—especially when a cold front passes, a host of boats zoom by or fishing pressure gets too heavy. This method also works when fishing in off-color to downright muddy water.

Flippin', a favorite underhand method used by many bass pros, can be part of the action. The trick is to get a minnow down into thick cover on heavy gear and then shake the cover by jerking the line. A typical rig might consist of a long flippin' stick or stout pole and 15- to 30-pound-test line, ending with a large dipsey sinker. An 8-inch-long dropper is placed a foot above the sinker, leading to a No. 2 to 4 or, with the big sucker baits, up to a 4/0. This is not "tiddler tackle!"

Present the bait as quietly as possible by lowering or flipping it. Feel the bait as it sinks on a slightly slack line. Gently move your rod up and down; don't bring the rod up past shoulder height—you'll lose the "sock 'em" power needed to set big hooks.

Being able to feel the action remains critical to this method's success. Experience (and sensitive fingers) tells you when the line or sinker touches cover and how the shaking process is going. Big fish will be drawn to such a disturbance if it's large enough to attract yet not threaten.

Flying Minnows

Kites have been used by saltwater anglers for years. Special waterproof kites skip baits away from the boat's wake. Shore fishermen grabbed onto the idea for those unfortunately few days when the wind blows offshore. Then, Florida's bass anglers started using kites rigged with a line release to carry big suckers and other large minnows well back into virtually inaccessible areas where weeds and lily pads grew thicker than deer hair. Muskie and pike fishermen picked up on the approach.

Two separate methods have evolved. One involves trolling a lip-hooked sucker or big minnow off of a kite behind a boat. This works when the wind is blowing over the boat toward the weeds or cover. With the second system, a kite is used from a stationary boat or from the bank to move baits downwind over apparently productive spots.

In either system a skipped bait is used; it's in the water and then, as you pull the kite string, on the surface and out of the water. This produces some rather spectacular baitfish action, which in turn should result in some spectacular strikes from big fish that become "turned on" by the baitfish's erratic behavior.

These systems call for heavy gear; 20- to 25-pound-test line seems to be the minimum. Add a short leader and a big hook impaled just below the dorsal fin for stationary methods; through the lips for trolling. The line from angler to kite is, of course, threaded onto a standard downrigger release or through an inexpensive rubber band. A sturdy rod and reel spooled with the same test line helps control the kite.

Still Water, Moving Minnows

Many of these methods involve jigs, spinners and the like. Cast and retrieved minnows work for bank and anchored boat anglers with plenty of bait; however, constant casting and retrieving, as opposed to casting and waiting, is hard on baitfish. Still, casting and slowly retrieving tough baits, like chubs, is particu-

North American Fisherman Editor Steve Pennaz tangled with this walleye while trolling a live minnow in a relatively shallow portion of a Canadian lake.

larly appropriate for "ambush" species, such as pike or muskies.

However, it's more effective to troll minnows where conditions permit. In-line sinkers with swivels ahead of a short leader work, as do trolling planes, downriggers, various "no snag" rigs, like Gapen's Bait Walkers, and sideplaners. Like lead-core and wire line, each offers advantages and disadvantages for use in bait trolling.

The sideplaner deserves special mention as a dandy way to move baits in front of boat- or wake-shy fish. Also you can keep your boat in deeper water while running your planer close to the bank. This can be very productive the morning after a storm has left battered bait on the windward shore of the lake. At such times, gamefish will be cruising in to munch on dead and injured baitfish.

River And Stream Presentations

You can either move your bait in an effort to put it in front of your targeted quarry or let it stay put so fish can follow its scent up to the hook. The decision hinges upon the activity level of the fish you are seeking.

When fish are in a migratory mode, such as salmon or steelhead hiding behind rocks or in deep pools, consider "plonking" or simply chucking your bait into the water and waiting for the action to develop.

Most still-water bait rigs work in holes. When minnows are fished in one spot in current, they should be lip-hooked; tail- or dorsal-fin hooked minnows tend to spin and twist the line. However, you should fish a minnow off a Wolf River or breakaway dropper setup in current so it spins attractively; a ball-bearing swivel reduces line twist.

Wolf River Rigs

Big flathead catfish eat monster minnows. Channels, blues, bullheads and other "whisker fish" also go for minnows.

Perhaps the best way to fish these big baits is by using the classic Wolf River rig, named for the Wolf River tailwaters where it

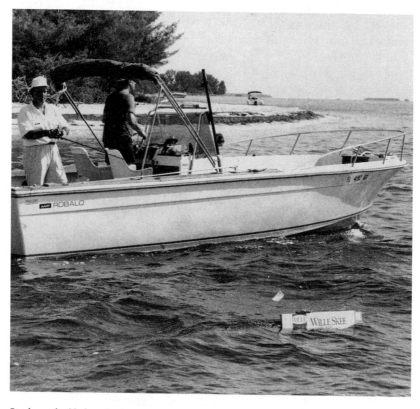

Single- or double-board sideplaners create greater lateral spread in bait presentations. They are also effective in dealing with boat-shy fish and in placing the bait in the shallowest water near shore.

Minnow, Baitfish Presentations

became popular. Actually, saltwater anglers will recognize this as the standard pyramid sinker and three-way swivel rig that is popular on most ocean beaches. The only real difference is the saltwater rig is designed to hang the sinker on the bottom to hold position in the sometimes mighty tidal currents. The heavier sinker is less likely to be swept along in the current.

The three-way swivel that's tied to the end of the line is the critical part of the rig. A 3-foot-long leader that's 25 percent lighter in test weight than the main line holds the bait. A 4-foot-long breakaway dropper that's 50 percent lighter than the main line carries the pyramid sinker.

Various hooking systems work. Traditionally, the minnow is threaded onto the leader and a fairly large treble (1/0 to 3/0) that's tied to the leader is pulled back into the bait. You can also use a whole minnow on a pinned double hook. Hooking minnows through the nose works only in slower currents because minnows tend to be cast off or are stripped off by strong currents. The pinned double hook secures the bait better.

Chuck this rig into roiling tailwaters among huge boulders or along undercut banks and hang on.

Rolling Mad Toms And Sculpins

These tiny baits all live tight to the bottom so that's where gamefish expect to find them. On snaggy bottoms various snag-resistant rigs work. But on gravel or cobble bottoms where trout and smallmouths lurk, a rolling bait seems to work best. It's a version of the Carolina rig, detailed in Chapter 7. At the end of a 2-foot-long leader is either a No. 4 or No. 6 short-shank bait hook in the bait's tail or a threaded-on double-pin hook. The former offers better action; the latter retains the bait on the hook better in heavy currents or during longer casts.

It's easy to fish these rigs downstream; however, it's more productive, although more work, to fish them at a 45-degree or greater angle upstream. Feathering the line with your finger during the cast eliminates slack that might snag your bait; close the bail as the bait hits the water and follow the bait with the rodtip. Reel in any slack.

When the bait reaches an angle of about 45 degrees downstream, reel in or open the bail to release line and control the drift until you've covered the run or pool. Retrieve at a slow enough

Rig For Irregular Bottoms

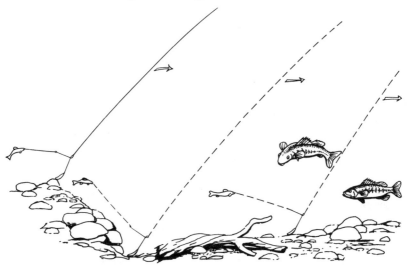

A rig utilizing a "walking" sinker keeps the bait in the proper position (just off an irregular bottom) yet prevents snagging on rocks or other structure.

rate so you don't damage your bait; cast again. Pay particular attention to likely spots, such as undercut banks or ledges, the shady sides of rocks and other choice fish-holding structure. It's important that the bait stays near the bottom, but does not hang up. Some fishermen nip the ends off the pectoral fins of Mad toms and sculpins so they can't hide in holes in the rocks. Too much weight can cause the same problem. If you can't go to a smaller size egg sinker, switch to split shot.

At dawn, dusk or after dark, big fish often herd minnows into the shallows where they are easy to catch. If you wade the shallows, you will scare these fish. Instead, wade down the middle of a waist- to chest-deep stream, casting to both banks. If you're bankbound, cast from well back up the bank. After you've covered the shallows, you can approach the water to cast farther out.

River Backtrolling

Boaters use the slip-sinker rig, Gapen's Bait Walker or another "no-snag" setup to backtroll for intensive coverage of river holes they know hold fish. (Anyone who has ever "Hot Shotted" for salmon or steelhead knows the method.) Using a set dropback

Minnow And Baitfish Preferences And Habitat

Species	Temperatures			Region and Habitat Type	Hardiness
	Lower	Ideal	Upper		
Alewife	48	54	72	Widespread in lakes	C
Chub, Bluehead	50	59	63	Streams east of the Rockies	H
Chub, Creek	45	50	55	Widespread - East	H
Chub, Lake	45	50	55	Widespread - Lakes	H
Chub, River	43	52	60	Rivers and streams	H
Dace, Blacknose	60	64	69	Fast streams, eastern U.S.	H
Dace, Finescale	55	61	68	Great Lakes—bogs/ streams/lakes	H
Dace, Redbelly	62	70	75	Small streams	H
Goldfish	70	78	90	Widespread—slow water	H
Minnows, Bluntnose	70	84	88	Eastern U.S.	H
Minnows, Fathead	65	73	85	Widespread	V
Shiners, Common	60	64	70	Streams and lakes	C
Shiners, Emerald	60	66	70	Eastern U.S.	Q
Shiners, Golden	65	70	75	Still waters, weeds, lakes	H
Shiners, Red	70	80	86	Large rivers	H
Shiners, Spottail	65	70	75	Slow and still waters	H

(V = very hardy, H = hardy, C = careful handling, Q = quickly dies)

A quick glance at this chart gives the angler an indication of the baitfish found in the same temperature zone as particular gamefish.

(Most use about 20 "pulls" or 60 feet of line out over the stern.) sinker big enough to tick the bottom without hanging up and executing proper boat-maneuvering (in which it moves back and forth across the current while slowly dropping back downstream) probes each and every bit of bottom.

Most experts agree that this can't be done too slowly. A 50-yard-long, 30-foot-wide hole might, for example, take 30 minutes to cover. It's too bad this is such an effective method; the only person who can stay awake is the one with the hand on the tiller. It's worse than watching cricket!

Matching Baits And Gamefish

Like gamefish, minnows and baitfish are more temperature conscious than most other baits. If you fish where the water temperature is optimum for both the bait and the gamefish, you will radically increase your success ratio. You should know when fish leave their "comfort zone" to savage bait in warmer water.

It's just as important to know what temperatures minnows and baitfish prefer as it is to know the targeted gamefish's preferences. If in doubt, fish where baitfish are active early or late in the day. Water in this temperature range may hold fewer gamefish; however, those that spot your bait will likely be hungry. Note also that aquatic insects hatch at specific temperatures and crayfish aren't active until water temperature rises past 50 degrees or so.

Temperature preferences are sometimes modified by habitat and climate. Fish at the northern end of their range, for example, seem comfortable and active at lower temperatures than do their brethren farther south. Conversely, fish in the South will tolerate hotter water. What's hot for a largemouth bass in Michigan might be just right for a Florida lunker.

Because water temperatures may vary during the day, use this knowledge to schedule your fishing excursions. When the water is at its warmest, fish at night or from dawn until the sun starts hitting the water. In cold weather, opt for afternoon and early evening fishing. Waters warm from lower elevations to higher elevations, so lakes and streams of the same size and type will always offer "hot" fishing in the same order up the hill in spring and down the hill in fall—even when dates may differ. Keep a log of this order and you will know when and where to be. (Remember that the shallows of lakes and streams with southern exposure will offer the best fishing in early spring.)

Amphibians
And Shellfish

=11=

Frogs, Toads, Salamanders

Frogs, toads and salamanders aren't as popular today as they once were. Perhaps Kermit the Frog is the reason. Clearly, little wiggling "hands" and "feet" produce squeamish reactions in some otherwise tough-as-nails anglers. If you overcome this, you can enjoy one of the best big-fish baits for bass, pike, walleyes, muskies or brown trout. If that were not the case, you wouldn't see so many frog-finished lures in the tackle shops. Catfish will take frogs all summer, too, and salamanders are always tasty treats for all large gamefish.

All amphibians need water in which to breed. In fact, the word *amphibian* is derived from the Greek word *amphibios* meaning "to live a double life." This reflects amphibians' ability to live on land and in water. Some species spend most of their time in the water. Others, like frogs and mole salamanders, spend some time in the water, but migrate to spend much of their life cycle on land. Almost all species hide; many are nocturnal, most are timid.

In most cases, amphibians are differentiated from their cousins, the reptiles, because of their moist skins and lack of claws. However, when collecting mole salamanders, keep in mind the markings on young venomous snakes native to your area.

Like their reptilian relatives, frogs, toads and salamanders are cold-blooded creatures that hibernate or go dormant when ambient temperature drops below 50 degrees Fahrenheit. However, all amphibians prefer temperatures below 70 degrees. They work best as bait from spring until fall in the North but may produce results

The toad (top), frog and mole salamander are representative of the many amphibian baits that are available to the serious angler. Although they are highly successful baits, they are not used in many areas.

Frogs, Toads, Salamanders

when used as bait throughout the year in the South.

Frogs And Toads

Frogs live and escape from predators in the water. Toads live on land in wet areas and stay out of harm's way in burrows. Frogs usually have smooth skin, long legs and the ability to jump. Toads usually have warty skin and can only hop. Frogs seem more bound to be near water and marshes. Some toads do well far from water and, when it is very dry, they can estivate—a process like hibernation—for considerable periods.

Toads and frogs are surprisingly vocal, and their calls can lead you to them. Neither species will give you warts, but toads do secrete some liquids that will make sensitive areas, such as eyes or lips, sting.

Frogs and toads start as a gummy mass of eggs laid in water. The hatch produces tadpoles, or larvae, with gills and long tails. The tadpoles' tails eventually are absorbed and they mature into adults. This process takes part of the summer; however, it takes two years for bull frogs. Mature frogs often move into bogs and meadows during the summer but return to deep lakes and ponds in the fall to overwinter before laying eggs the next spring in the warm shallows. The fall migration leads frogs into the shallows where northern pike and walleyes lurk following fall turnover. You don't want to miss this event because easy limits can be the result.

Species And Habitat

Most species of frogs and toads work great as bait, even though few frog species ever see fish hooks. The green, leopard (with round spots) and pickerel (with square spots) are the most common frog baits west of the Rocky Mountains. They don't grow very large, are widely distributed and seem fairly easy to raise. It does help to know a bit about the lifestyles of the frogs that you fish so you can fish them properly and be able to find them if you're collecting them as bait.

The most common types of frogs are covered in the following paragraphs.

Bull, Green, Pickerel, Leopard And Crayfish Frogs: Most of these look like the frogs you chased, caught and played with as a kid. Given those memories, it's hard to explain the decline in the use

Live frogs are a good bait for a number of gamefish. They can be hooked through the lip like minnows or through a leg. Leg-hooked frogs create the most realistic action.

of these interesting baits. For whatever reason, frog bait use is down in most of the country, and never did seem that popular in the West. This seems strange because of the high percentage of artificials available in frog finish that produce well. Natural baits, then, should be even better on pike, pickerel and other large predatory fish because the chances of meeting a big fish that hasn't seen a live, as opposed to an artificial, frog are up. The fish should pulverize your amphibian!

As always, a bait-to-gamefish size match helps. Only optimistic muskie and pike fishermen and those who seek huge southern bass should try these big frogs whole; it's claimed that frogs eat small fish and eggs from bass nests, too.

Big bull, river and pig frogs seem better as cut bait. Green frogs run from bright green through olive drab to brown to match their

Green frogs are often used as bait throughout their largely Eastern habitat. They range in color from bright green to olive to brown, matching the varying colors of their habitat.

mostly Eastern habitat. Look for these in clear streams, creeks and ponds. Carpenter frogs stick to Eastern coastal plain bogs where their brown color blends into the sphagnum moss and tea-colored water. Pickerel frogs and the similar leopard frogs are widely distributed on the East Coast in bogs, swamps and, in the case of leopard frogs, on grasslands. As you might expect from the name, pickerel frogs are popular baits for pickerel and pike. Crayfish frogs represent targets of opportunity for crayfish collectors because they live in the flooded, abandoned crayfish holes.

Chorus And Tree Frogs: These dandy little frogs aren't used much for bait because they are difficult to find when they hide around ponds. Spring peepers, a host of chorus-frog species, and tree frogs run from 1 to 2 inches in length. Tree frogs can even change color! They are wonderful baits for brown trout and not bad for pickerel.

Trying Tadpoles

Few anglers use tadpoles as bait because they are delicate and often difficult to keep on the hook. Tadpoles do, however, attract all sorts of gamefish. If you keep casting to a minimum in order to reduce bait damage, it's not impossible to fish tadpoles. Put a sharp No. 8 wire Aberdeen hook gingerly through the tadpole's lips. When tadpoles are nearly mature, the hook can be inserted behind their developing legs. Hooks with wire ties also work. Tadpoles, like small pickerel or green frogs, seem particularly good bait for big brown trout.

Tadpoles are most effective early in the summer when small frogs have just barely emerged from their tadpole waters. Many tadpole species have disappeared by midsummer. However, if you raise tadpoles in tanks and regulate the light duration or select bullfrog tadpoles that take longer to mature, you will be able to use these baits all year long.

Finding Frogs

Finding frogs isn't difficult if you know where to look. Methods of catching frogs and toads range from the sporting—using a

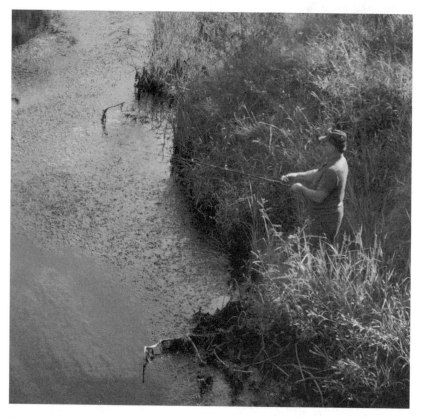

Water like this is not only a good spot to find panfish and bass, but is also a likely home for tadpoles in the spring and early summer. They are easily found in locations like this.

Frogs, Toads, Salamanders

fly rod and a large ragged fly to hook bullfrogs—to simply picking them up along paths, roads or mowed grassy areas near water. This also makes a nice outing for children.

If you're trying to catch frogs by hand, a pair of the "sure grip" gloves that have nubs on the palms will improve your grasp. Bull-frogs will play "possum" when caught. They go limp, and just when you get ready to bag them, they leap to safety. Do not introduce bullfrogs to waters where they aren't already present; these big bullies tend to replace other species.

When collecting tree and other small frogs, a small minnow or landing net helps pin down these quick little critters. Smaller green frogs fit nicely into the little dip nets sold in pet stores. For most other species, a long-handled landing net can provide the extra reach you will need to nab frogs perched in awkward-to-reach places.

Dyeing your net mesh brown by soaking it in a tea solution makes it much easier to catch frogs than using a white net bag. Painting the net rim and handle a dull brown or green improves gamefish netting percentages, too. Dull-colored nets help reduce your chances of losing fish at boatside.

Floating in a boat or tube at night along lily pads or near the bank is a great way to catch amphibian baits. Frog eyes shine when hit by a light and the spotlighted frogs usually remain frozen in place until netted.

Buying And Caring For Amphibian Bait

When buying bait frogs and toads, make sure they are lively and have no obvious defects, such as gig holes or broken limbs. Overcrowding in containers seems to cause the most problems. As always, you can tell a decent commercial bait operation by its smell and the general housekeeping. Good frog containers include wire-mesh enclosures if properly shaded, commercial frog boxes and Styrofoam and other types of coolers. All containers should have 1 to 2 inches of water; pebbles, rocks or broken crockery, which frogs climb on to get out of the water, and a lid. Toad containers are much the same, except with less water and more sand and gravel. Frogs and toads are both durable baits if you don't subject them to too many casts. You need to keep them wet and shaded. As noted earlier, overcrowding can be a major problem. (Frogs will let you know if this happens; they develop redleg, with

Complete Angler's Library

Mudpuppies And Sirens

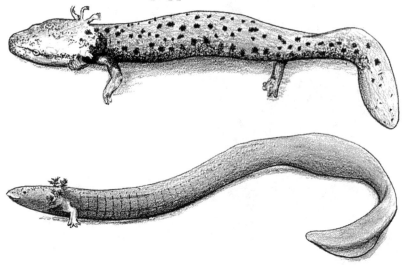

The mudpuppy (top) and the siren are two highly successful baits that live in shallow, stagnant and often warm water. Sirens are a very durable bait offering a snake-like action in the water.

characteristic symptoms of red belly blotches.) As a rule, 2 inches of frogs per gallon of container is quite safe.

All sorts of live bugs will keep frogs frisky. Crickets work nicely, as well as meal worms and various insect larvae. Dead insects don't work for amphibians; they should be removed from cages daily. Change water in the container at least once a week. If you can't catch frog food, use grubs or purchase frog food from a pet shop. Dead frogs should be removed from the container immediately and frozen in water to be used later for catfish bait.

Salamanders

Well over 100 species of salamanders can be found in North America. These baits present a confusion of choices during the warmer water months of late spring, summer and early fall. Species identification is quite important because collection and keeping methods vary by type. Even if you buy your bait, you should be sure you get what you pay for.

Giant salamanders include real waterdogs, mudpuppies and the incredibly durable sirens. All live in usually shallow, generally stagnant and often warm water. All have external gills, the classic

Frogs, Toads, Salamanders

A waterdog is an excellent bait for many gamefish species. This bait is usually lip-hooked. It should be stored at no more than 50 degrees in order to slow the maturation process.

field mark. Sirens, one of the most popular baits, look more like eels with minuscule front legs. These superb baits usually aren't found in shops, but they offer such a wonderful snake-like action that they seem well worth the effort to catch and keep.

Look for lungless salamanders, such as the spring lizards which are easy to collect when in season yet difficult to find otherwise, in damp woods, along moving waters. Their skinny bodies and large hind legs are fairly good field marks. Transport them to holding containers in a bucket that is about half full of damp—not wet—leaf mold.

Mole salamanders, as you might expect, burrow like moles in damp soil. Like nightcrawlers, they emerge on wet nights. The most popular bait in this group is the "waterdog" in larval form. A continuous fin above and below the rear of the body and undeveloped legs are good field marks. An easy bait to grow, it remains the most popular amphibious bait for those who seek bass, pike and other big gamefish.

Giant salamanders can be caught on hooks baited with worms. In the spring, use a bobber rig for panfish to keep your bait out of the salamander's reach. Giant sirens can run up to a yard in length, so only the young work well for most gamefish.

Ditches, marsh areas and drainage canals around rice fields are

Complete Angler's Library

good habitat for sirens. By floating a wire-mesh box and sorting through weeds, you will collect all sorts of other baits, such as aquatic insects, too.

In the South, the roots of water hyacinth offer ideal habitat for sirens. In the North, riverside channels and sloughs with underwater vegetation offer ideal habitat for mudpuppies and real waterdogs.

An old piece of window screen nailed or stapled onto the bottom of a 2-by-3-foot frame of 2-by-4 lumber that's held together by drywall screws works with coarser weeds, such as water hyacinth. A second box with 1/4-inch wire mesh works better with fine weeds, at the price of losing most aquatic insects and other small baits. Drop small plastic, covered boxes into each corner of the screened frame so you have containers for the collected bait.

Slip-Bobber Rigs For Panfish

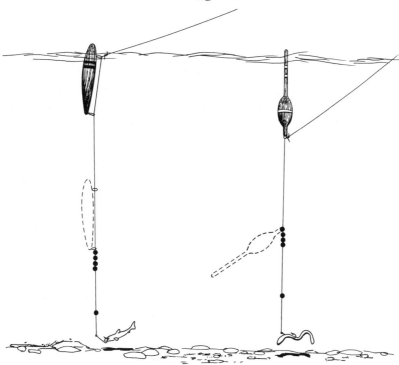

Slip-bobber rigs such as the two in this illustration work well for panfish, and when properly tuned will keep the bait up out of the reach of sirens and crayfish.

Frogs, Toads, Salamanders

Spotted bass love spring lizards, or lungless salamanders. These salamanders are easily caught in the spring because they hide under objects and are slow-moving.

Spring Lizards, Lungless Salamanders And Waterdogs

Lungless salamanders, such as spring lizards, move fast so your best bet is to catch them with a flashlight and a long-handled net. You can also catch them with an artificial fly on a short leader off the tip of a fly rod.

Mole salamanders are so easy to find during the spring that many fishermen collect a season's supply after the first spring rains. As is the case with frogs, searching around ponds at night does the job. During the day, these slow-moving morsels should be easy to catch by turning over rocks, stones and boards and grabbing them as they try to move to cover.

Larval tiger salamanders, also known as waterdogs, seine up like minnows in spring ponds, ditches and other areas where gamefish can't get to them. The larvae of other mole salamanders also work. Transfer all of these into keeping tanks in water-filled buckets.

Don't worry if you can't identify everything that turns up in your net. Colors vary widely, and many regional differences—subspecies—causing experts to squabble over the fine points. Fish don't care!

Complete Angler's Library

Salamanders will survive just about anything except becoming too dry. They also can manage for months without food. Big ones can be fed minnows or worms and small ones will eat items such as brine shrimp from the pet shop.

Giant salamanders, larval tiger salamanders and true waterdogs store best in 50-degree (F) water that's changed at least every five days. Water warmer than 50 degrees turns larval waterdogs into adults faster than you might like. As in the case of frogs, you can control maturation with temperature control to some extent.

Sirens can handle water temperatures of up to 75 degrees. Spring lizards and mole salamanders are best kept at 45 degrees in a covered container half full of aged leaf mold. All species need fairly frequent sorting. Throw out any fatalities or freeze them for use later as dead bait.

=12=

Crustaceans Of All Kinds

Gamefish have little trouble gobbling small crustaceans. They develop this skill early by dining on zooplankton and quickly graduating to miniature crusty baits, such as scuds. As they grow, they catch crayfish or crabs on the molt and even manage to down hardshells. Some gamefish species, like redear sunfish—known as shellcrackers in the South—or drum, specialize in crunching and munching clams, mussels and snails. Most will happily lunch on bashed crustacean and shellfish targets of opportunity.

Shrimp offer few problems for bait anglers. Bait shrimp include both fresh- and saltwater species—the former with longer legs and antennae—and grass shrimp that live in both marine and freshwater weeds. Mud shrimp, which are really a burrowing softshell crab, offer something different, and are incredibly effective for steelhead and salmon. Given these choices, as well as their easy handling and keeping, you can see why these crustaceans are so popular. The biggest problem, perhaps, with shrimp and crayfish is whether you want to use them as bait or fix them for dinner!

Admittedly, some are a problem to keep on the hook; others are difficult to obtain. Species like freshwater shrimp, for example, are not always commercially available; other baits, such as scuds, are uncommon in bait shops. However, tests indicate that all types of shrimp are prime bait for most species, and properly rigged scuds can't be beat for trout. With the West Coast's addic-

This largemouth bass had feasted on a crayfish before being caught. Crayfish are a favorite food for largemouths.

Crustaceans Of All Kinds

tion for mud shrimp and shucked crayfish tails as steelhead baits, it's strange that more bait shops haven't jumped into the action.

Like all underwater creatures, however, crustaceans are stuck in rather narrow environmental slots including bottom type, current speed and, in some cases, water pH. Present these baits where they naturally occur and you will catch more fish.

Crayfish: An Extraordinary Bait

Crayfish, a species of freshwater, spiny lobster, obviously are not fish. Their name is an English phonetic translation of the old German term *krebiz*, which is a variation of the word *krebs*, or crab. Whether they are called krebiz, crayfish, crawdads (Southern term) or ecrevisse (French term), these dandy baits tempt all sorts of gamefish ranging from big brown trout to lunker largemouths to monster pike. Many anglers think there is no better bait for smallmouth bass. (The popularity of crayfish finishes on artificial lures attest to this). Anglers should fish crayfish on the shady side of the hole, stream or rock, near the bank or under the trees. Using crayfish bait at dusk, dawn or during the night should improve the success ratio even more.

If possible, you should buy shedders, or soft crayfish, that have just molted; they are prime baits. Paper shells, the next stage in the crayfish's development of the usual armor plating, are the next best. In either case, make sure the crayfish are lively. Good bait candidates are the ones that back up and wave their claws in a menacing manner when threatened by the bait seller's net. Those that will likely expire soon don't move much. To keep crayfish lively, give them sufficient room in storage and bait containers. Keep them in a cooler full of water until needed or stash them in wet leaves or paper for very short periods.

Crayfish grow best and biggest in limestone streams, ponds and rocky lakes. Because most of these clawed critters are nocturnal, concentrate on lake banks or streams that run east and west or have several trees. Crayfish stay out later in the morning and come out of burrows or from under rocks later in the afternoon. To get them out, simply tempt them with food.

There are several ways to catch crayfish. The commercial solution is a wire-mesh trap baited with whatever is handy and cheap—pork or other liver is good—and placed where current will carry the food smell to these critters. Most traps are left overnight

Crayfish are relatively easy to catch, and it doesn't take fancy equipment to do it. A weighted strip of bacon dangled from a dried branch often does the job. Crayfish can be caught on standard fishing tackle, too.

and emptied every day. This remains the best method for still-water fishing too.

It is more challenging to catch crayfish in moving water. Trophy hunters dangle a weighted strip of bacon in likely spots along rocky or undercut banks. With polarized sunglasses, you can spot crayfish hiking upstream to your bait during the day. You should wait until the crayfish seizes the bait. Then, pick the bait off the bottom and slide a net underneath it. Teenagers and compulsive types try to catch crayfish on the fly by placing a net behind them and prodding them with a stick. (When startled, crayfish move backward.) They can also be caught on fishing tackle.

Crayfish can be kept in a bucket of cool water that is shaded if the water is aerated frequently. If you plan to eat the biggest ones you catch, changing the water several times and adding a little

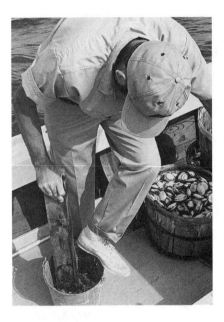

Soft-shell clams can be ground up for use as chum for striped bass. Pieces of shell and the clams' fluids act as an attractant for stripers and other gamefish.

cornmeal to the container helps remove the mud. This also works for shellfish.

Soft-Shelled Crayfish

Like lobsters and crabs, crayfish must shed their shells periodically as they outgrow them. After this occurs, it takes a while for the new carapace to harden. During this period, then, crayfish hide under rocks and in burrows. Crayfish start as hardshells; then, early in the molt, they become "peelers." When the old shell is gone, the crayfish becomes a "soft shell." In a day or so, shells harden and you have a "paper shell." While this is happening, crayfish, recognizing their vulnerability, stay under rocks or in burrows where fish can't get at them. Obviously, most fish consider the soft and paper shells a great delicacy. In some parts of the country, savvy bait sellers collect crayfish, feed them until they're stuffed and molting and then sell the soft shells for a premium price. These crayfish may be the best baits for those who night-fish for brown trout or go after smallmouth.

Crayfish techniques also work with brackish water crabs, such as blue crabs and smaller hermit crabs, and other species commonly used as bait in freshwater. All work well on basic crayfish rigs in appropriate waters. You can pick up hermit crabs along the

Complete Angler's Library

water's edge at low tide, net them off gravel or sand bottoms or, where legal, harvest them from tidepools. Mud and a number of other crab species can be caught in nets and preserved in wet seaweed or weeds for several hours.

Opinions vary concerning removal of crayfish and crab claws. It doesn't seem to make much difference because most crayfish recovered from smallmouth bass still have pinchers intact.

Shrimp Are Excellent Bait, Too

Live marine and freshwater shrimp hooked through the collar or the tail are excellent bait for most freshwater gamefish and a host of species, such as black or striped bass that move between saltwater and freshwater. Freshwater shrimp, which are common in the South and range up to 8 or 9 inches in length, work well as

Shrimp tails, as well as other shrimp portions, can be used effectively. At top left, a tail is threaded over a snelled hook; at right, a piece of shrimp is threaded onto another single hook.

bait. Smaller saltwater shrimp, as well as fresh- and saltwater grass shrimp, take fish, too. As bait, all of these species seem interchangeable.

Considering the price of shrimp, you may want to catch your own. Serious coastal anglers tow miniature versions of commercial shrimp seines. Others set out wire-mesh shrimp traps, baited with fish scraps. More active anglers shine lights on the water and net the responding shrimp from a boat, or they will sweep their long-handled nets through the water under pier lights in both fresh- and saltwater.

A simple baited net tied to a rope works, too. An old bicycle rim attached to the open end of a gunny sack is as simple as it gets. The "net" is baited with a can of fish-flavored cat food so it can attract a lot of shrimp and not trap thieves. These simple nets can be set in spots with little current for an hour or two, or they can be left out overnight. Some species of shrimp are nocturnal so bait collecting after dark can be effective. These species will eat your bait and, in many cases, avoid daylight by hiding in the dark folds of your sacking trap.

Grass shrimp can be shaken out of weeds, harvested with a special roller-bottom push net or raked out of eel grass with a wire garden rake. Store these like other shrimp and save some damp eel grass as packing material.

Mud shrimp, like the West Coast ghost shrimp or larger blue mud shrimp, will catch steelhead and salmon as far as 300 miles from saltwater. These, along with live herring, are prime bait for sturgeon, too. Mud shrimp are a popular and effective bait that are also found on the Gulf Coast.

Harvesting mud shrimp adds a new definition to the word *dirty*. Even though you can dig them off sand and mud flats at low tide with a shovel, you will do better using either a clam tube or shrimp gun. The first step is to tell the difference between clam and mud shrimp burrows. The latter are about an inch in diameter and seem more regular in outline. When you find one, insert the clam tube, twist it while covering the air hole at the top and pull up. When you uncover the air hole, the contents will drop out of the tube. Shrimp and clams are easy to sort, but be sure to carry enough containers so that they don't become crowded.

Shrimp guns are like a big suction tube and are easily made. They work like clam tubes, except that you pull up a plunger to suck the shrimp into the tube. Push the contents out of the tube and collect your shrimp.

Securing Scuds

In many streams and lakes, scuds—a tiny freshwater shrimp never larger than an inch—are a favorite food for trout. Collecting these is as easy as shaking weeds over a floating box or net.

You can also slosh weeds about in a bucket or, better yet, a white Styrofoam cooler to collect scuds, dobsonfly larvae. The background of the white bucket helps you see these and other tiny baits. A wire-mesh box also helps in sorting.

Scuds, like freshwater shrimp, live in weeds. You should fish them in channels and holes. As a rule, deeper seems better with scuds. While mud shrimp don't keep well, scuds keep very well in an aquarium because of their small size. Remember that they aren't sick when they swim on their sides!

Mussels And Clams

Shellfish appeal to more freshwater gamefish than one might expect. Clams and mussels are more widely distributed in lakes, rivers and ponds than most anglers realize. Shellfish appear in some isolated waters because birds carry their larval forms. Free-swimming or drifting larvae move long distances, too.

Estuarine gamefish, as well as freshwater drum, sturgeons, landlocked striped bass, catfish, panfish and even trout eat marine clams and mussels. The problem, for the fish, is getting the clams open. Sturgeons accomplish this with their grinding plates. Other species must make do with scraps from natural attrition.

Selecting Shellfish

Fresh clams and mussels aren't sold far from saltwater or catfish action. If you buy shellfish for bait or the table, insist that shells are closed tightly. If you tap the shellfish and it doesn't close, pick another in better shape.

It's nice that shellfish are easy to glean from sand, gravel, mud or even rocks. If you see empty shells, move upcurrent. You'll find mussels or clams busily filtering out particulate matter.

Picking Your Own

Gathering shellfish can be as easy as picking them up after

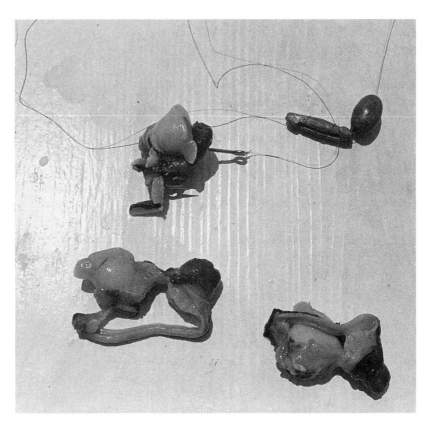

Clams are also a good bait. The meat can be used with a typical bottom rig with sinkers and a single hook. The clam's juices are a successful attractant.

you've felt them in the soft bottom. Some, however, use a garden rake to cull baits.

You can even track them in the sand by the curving path they leave on the bottom. It's important not to take too many on your fishing trip. If you break some, use them immediately or bring them along for chum. Collecting shellfish where you plan to fish is a good idea; the mud and munchies you stir up will attract fish to the area from downstream or downcurrent. If you use a mussel or clam as bait, you can expect action.

Some small clams are scattered in sand and easiest to gather in a mesh-bottomed, wood frame. Mussels stick tight to rocks but can be pulled off by rocking them toward the curved side of their shell. Or, simply pry them up with a geologist's pick or hammer. River mussels used whole are decent catfish baits. Strips of muscle or the tough fringes of the mantle can be cut into solid panfish bait and jig "sweeteners." Zebra mussels make dandy chum.

Once you've caught your shellfish, they require a bucket full of clean, cool water for a couple days' storage. A wire cage—sometimes made by wiring together two plastic, milk containers—hung off a dock for a season keeps clams contented and mussels mellow.

Opening clams is easy if you slip a thin-bladed knife along the side and cut the muscle—the firm part that's the best bait for small fish—in half. It's wise not to open clams or mussels until they are needed as bait, unless you're after catfish which prefer clams that are rather "off." Shucking over the water in which you're fishing allows the retained liquid in the shellfish to attract fish.

Snails And Slugs

Only a few fishermen realize that slugs and, if you shuck them, standard garden snails will be gobbled up by most gamefish. Aquatic snails, like those that give the shellcracker its name, offer more treats for gamefish. In brackish water, tasty items, like turban snails, work, too.

You can collect snails and slugs by setting a saucer of beer in the garden at night and harvesting the "drunk bunch" in the morning. It's even easier to make friends with an organic gardener who handpicks slugs rather than nuking them with pesticides. Slugs will keep in damp torn newspaper or on worm bedding and, as gardeners know, happily munch on leaves.

Aquatic snails can be picked off the bottom. Make sure to use them with an appropriate-sized hook—No. 8 to 10 works best for most. Keep them on weeds in a bucket of water, an aquarium or tank. Bottom rigs are well-suited to these baits.

=13=

Smorgasbord Of Rigs And Methods

Conventional rigs and approaches outlined in this chapter will by no means exhaust the possibilities with baits that creep, crawl, peep or pinch. Most minnow rigs also work with amphibians. Worm rigs suit shrimp, and aquatic-insect rigs do a good job when tiny scuds are substituted as bait. However, there are rigs and methods that favor different types of bait. The objective is, of course, to present the bait—whether it be a crayfish, salamander or a snail—in the most natural way possible. With that in mind, let's look at some common setups on a species-by-species basis.

Fishing With Toads And Frogs

Frogs and toads provide a lively chunk of protein perfectly designed to attract predatory fish, particularly pike, muskies and largemouth bass. Just hook a frog through the small of the hind leg with a No. 4 or No. 2 hook attached to 15- or 20-pound-test line. Cast to a likely spot and feed line as you let the frog swim toward shore or the bottom—and hang on. Few other methods work as well from boats. This is because frogs seem to swim to shore. Of course, frogs fished in this manner on poles took largemouth bass long before baitcasting reels became popular.

Fishing a frog on a Wolf River rig can produce some large pike, catfish or muskies during hot summer days. After dark, the Wolf River rig with a frog under a large, lighted bobber works well at the slack-water end of pools.

If you're fishing with toads or frogs for larger gamefish species, such as pike, you'll want to use a little heavier tackle like the baitcasting outfits and the spinning outfit (center) shown here.

Smorgasbord Of Rigs And Methods

"Flinging frogs" is a descriptive name for another effective method. A No. 2 or larger hook is run from the frog's throat up through both lips, and the hook is tied to some 25-pound-test line fastened to a stout cane or fiberglass pole. This allows you to fish two rod lengths from your boat, float tube or wading spot.

In really heavy cover, use less line with a pole so you can carefully place your frog in an open spot within the weed or lily-pad mass. Then stroke the rig down to the bottom for four or five minutes; repeat this process in other likely cover, such as treetops or under sunken logs. When it's so hot worms fry on your boat deck, try frog flinging after dark.

Mr. Peepers

Small frogs—like inch-long peepers—attract a number of smaller gamefish species. Small trout, river smallmouths, walleyes and other medium-sized fish munch such baits if they are properly presented on 6- to 8-pound-test line and a No. 6 or 8 hook. This is effective in backwaters, stream inlets on natural lakes and, as soon as frogs come out in the spring, marshy shallows.

Basic Crayfish Rigs

Nothing is simpler than the basic crayfish rig for use on firm sand or gravel bottom. Put a No. 4 light-wire hook through the critter's tail (use a No. 6 hook for crayfish less than 3 inches long), add a split shot for casting weight, if needed, and you're set. The hook can also be strapped to the crayfish's middle with a rubber band; it lasts a bit longer. A No. 2, 4, 6 or 8 Aberdeen hook that is the same length as your bait's body works well.

Some anglers put the hook through the back of the shell. This works if you suspend the bait under a big bobber over extremely soft bottom so the bait won't burrow out of sight. Again, a rubber band or tie keeps crayfish livelier longer. Otherwise, stick with the tail-hook approach because savvy gamefish know enough to grab crayfish from the end opposite of the pinchers.

For moving crayfish over soft bottoms where they might otherwise disappear, use a Carolina sinker rig with a floating jig head hooked into the crayfish's tail. Using a slow retrieve allows the floating jig to force the crayfish up where it can be seen by fish attracted to the area by the mud puffs created by the sinker during the retrieve.

This hybrid bass found a soft or papershell crayfish too tempting to pass up. If it's rigged on a dropper line, the crayfish cannot bury itself under rocks and bottom debris.

On a fairly level bottom, the crayfish should be rigged on a 12-inch dropper set 18 inches above a cluster of terminal shot heavy enough to partly submerge a small bobber. Set the bait-to-bobber depth so the bobber movement causes the shot to drag, sending up "mud signals." In very slow current, this presentation can draw fish from a long distance.

Fishing "Three-Alarm" Sirens

In reasonably open water, put a No. 2 hook through the back of a 6-inch-long siren and freeline the bait like a frog. Follow the bait with the rodtip, giving it plenty of slack, and hold on.

A big bobber or one that is homemade from a coated juice carton provides more bait control when needed. This keeps your bait from hiding on the bottom.

Sirens troll well at slow speeds if partly pinned on double hooks behind a June bug or some other slow-turning spinner. Start impaling the hook about halfway back on the siren and let it come out of the siren's mouth. The hook should be attached to a spring-fastening, in-line spinner. Troll slowly along the outer edge of weedlines for bass or pike.

Fishing Spring Lizards

In big waters over uneven bottoms, a spring lizard hooked close to the rear legs on a Wolf River rig works well or, where the bottom is more even, try an egg sinker fish-finder rig. In very slow current or still water, oversized bobber rigs are a good choice.

For big brown trout running upstream to spawn, a freelined spring lizard can be one of the best baits. Spring lizards are also taken by post-spawn steelhead in some areas. They are also good baits for smallmouths, largemouths and pike.

Fishing Waterdogs

Nothing beats waterdogs as bait for big walleyes during the slack days of summer when walleyes sulk or suspend. All sorts of rigs enjoy regional favor. Super hooks that grip the waterdog at the neck with barbs rigged on a sliding sinker rig are used in the Upper Midwest. They extend bait life.

In other parts of the country, anglers use a baiting needle to thread waterdogs on like minnows. Most use a big treble hook. This, like the trailing hook used when short hits are a problem, improves hookup and hang-up percentages. A lighter double hook, with points up, will take as many fish with fewer snags.

Fishing Fresh- And Saltwater Shrimp

Shrimp rigs aren't complex. Most worm rigs used with and without bobbers also work for fresh- and saltwater shrimp. Special popping-cork floats, which are popular in tidal waters for using noise to attract species such as sea trout, work well, too. Or, you can use a big popping plug trailing an 18-inch-long dropper and a No. 4 hook baited with shrimp. A cautious, sidearm cast helps preserve the bait.

Grass shrimp, a particularly good panfish bait, perform well if threaded onto light-wire, No. 8 hooks or, in the case of very picky fish, through the back with a light-wire No. 10 or No. 12 hook.

A piece of shrimp or its tail can be threaded on a hook and fished with an egg-shaped slip sinker. The shrimp piece can be cast easily, and the fish won't feel resistance when a slip sinker is used.

Use the smallest possible shot 6 inches up the line and just a big enough bobber for casting weight. You can also fish grass shrimp without weight on ultra-light spinning gear or, by moving up to 12- or 15-pound-test line, in weedbed pockets with a cane pole. With baits like shrimp that are difficult to cast because of a lack of weight, double up by using two dropper loops. If you like, combine shrimp and a marine worm in brackish water or shrimp and a nightcrawler in freshwater. With so many fish being color sensitive, shrimp dyed red or green with a shot of food coloring in their holding water may be even more effective.

Although mud shrimp are really a species of softshell crab, they produce best if rigged on a tail hook like other shrimp. Just add a tie—rubber band or soft wire—to hold their long, rather limp bodies on a long-shanked hook. It seems odd that salmon and steelhead hit these baits hundreds of miles from saltwater, making some feel that this is a "memory bite" for steelhead or salmon harking back to their life in saltwater. For whatever reason, mud shrimp are prime bait for big steelhead, salmon, stripers and catfish.

Mud shrimp, when fished in rivers or tidewaters, are best used on fish-finder rigs. Run a big plastic-worm hook through the center of the shrimp's body and either stitch on the tail with a needle and thread, as done with a mooching rig, or use a No. 8 rubber band to hold the tail on. Make sure that the bait isn't able to move much.

Because mud shrimp are so delicate, many boaters will anchor upstream from their target and drift the shrimp downstream rather than casting it. Bobbers work well in very slow currents and where the bottom is even.

An easy sidearm toss decreases your chance of losing the bait. For the smoothest possible release, use a shallow "U" sidearm cast with the line pinned against the reel by the tip of your forefinger and released gently so the bait isn't jerked. To control spinning line slack, gently feather the line against your finger—never the spool—as it spins off the reel. When the bait hits the water, close the bail and you are ready for a strike immediately.

Selective Scuds

Scuds, which are delicate, require using the sidearm cast. Few baits work so well for trout and panfish. In fishing very clear Western waters, you'll do best using ultra ultra-light tackle—lines and leaders of 2-pound-test or lighter and No. 12 to No. 16 hooks (No. 20 for smaller scuds). These hooks will hold one, two, three or more scuds. Add the smallest shot you have a foot or so up the line and you're set. (If you don't have enough casting weight, a glob of mud or clay pinched in around the shot adds weight for casting that disperses and, in some cases, attracts fish upon entering the water.)

When you fish scuds in still water on calm days, the most delicate bobber available improves your chances. Often when trout aren't biting well, they will cruise in, nip the bait and, more often than not, release it. A tiny bobber in still water signals the first touch, allowing you to snap the hook home in time. One of the most effective rigs involves the use of a self-cocking bobber with a

Mini-Bobber Rig For Scuds

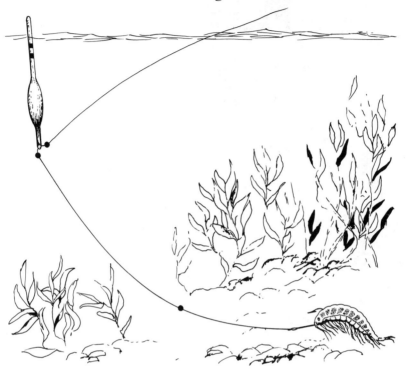

In current, scuds are best fished under a properly weighted mini-bobber. Scuds are easily lost when casting, so delicate handling is warranted.

wire stem, weighted down to the indicator line with shot squeezed on the stem, that lets the scud drift slowly down. This method can make a critical difference with picky trout. If the water is a bit rough, try using a windcheater rig with scuds as bait on one hook and something a bit more durable, like worms or a salmon egg, on the other.

Moving-water scuds work best under mini-bobbers. If you fish downstream, you may not need to add weight if you use a gentle sidearm cast or a long rod to put your bobber setup in the right drift line. Because scuds tend to cast off, such in-line, downstream drifts work well. As an alternative, consider using a wet fly tipped with a scud sweetener or a double-bait rig with something like a hellgrammite so you don't waste precious drift time in compensating for lost-bait casts.

A clams-digging excursion is a worthwhile effort. Clam meat is always a good bait for many gamefish, and the shells can be crushed and used as chum.

Fishing Clams And Mussels

Clams and mussels should be presented on the bottom. Big fish, like sturgeon, striped bass or monster catfish, deserve 2/0 or larger hooks and a whole clam, soft parts and all, for bait; big fish will munch whole clams. Soft parts of the clam will stay on better if they are wrapped in a piece of cheesecloth, a 4-inch-square piece of nylon stocking or with some self-adhesive thread used for fishing roe. You can, at least in the case of attracting catfish, improve clam durability by drying shucked clams in the sun until you can't stand the smell.

Crayfish and other pests eat shellfish baits, too. Some fishermen tie on a small float between the sinker and bait to keep clams and mussels slightly off the bottom. A threaded-on, tiny, commercial-made cork body used particularly for steelhead or a section of a wine cork that is slit and slid on the line is all that is needed to present shellfish just off the bottom.

Panfish and, yes, trout will take clams and mussels nicely on No. 8 hooks. (The tough section of the muscle that holds the shell shut is presented.) Yellow perch seem particularly fond of clams in the fall and winter. Considering the number of zebra mussels available in American waters, it's clear that there are bait and chumming opportunities beyond count.

Snails And Slugs

Slugs fresh from munching in the garden take a variety of fish; shucked garden snails work, too. Texture varies. Some slugs and snails are so soft that they won't stay on the hook. Slugs and snails from rural areas seem rather more athletic. Try setting a No. 6 hook in the tail and fish these critters along meadowed stream banks and lakes, using just a float for casting weight.

For those patient enough to collect aquatic snails by winnowing weeds over a floating screen and picky enough to carefully crack shells, such snails are a wonderful, albeit tiny, bait best fished around weedbeds. As with shellfish, carry them in a container and crack them in the boat. Use any bits and pieces and leftover liquid as chum.

A host of other marine and estuarine shellfish make fine bait. The moon shell, a huge snail that preys on clams, may have the toughest body of all. When cut into strips it's a winner for taking panfish. Whelks, limpets, turban snails and other shellfish all take catfish, panfish and other species.

Insect Baits

=14=

Aquatic Insects

Gamefish eat more pounds of aquatic insects than any other bait. "Water bugs" are only outweighed by algae in nature's pyramidal food chain that begins with simple single cell plants. As the number of members decreases at each level of the pyramid, the complexity of each organism increases. Starting at the bottom and working up, the pyramid includes the following organisms: zooplankton, aquatic insects, minnows and baitfish, gamefish and successful predators, such as man, animals and birds. As a result, you can't beat water bugs for sheer bait volume.

Aquatic insects go through more changes than a politician in an election year. They start as eggs laid in water and move through a number of aquatic nymph or larval stages. As in the case of a snake, an aquatic insect's skin isn't flexible. So, in order to grow, they must shed their skin anywhere from four to over 40 times before they hatch into their winged adult form. A few, such as caddis flies or craneflies, have an intermediate stage in which they build an underwater case, called a pupae, before hatching. Some aquatic insects hatch in water; others hatch on shores or in shoreline vegetation. Some survive for a day, week or month; others die after mating, and the dead flies (spinners) litter the stream. The density of such hatches results in astonishing concentrations of food that attract even big brown trout which normally eat "meat" like minnows or crayfish.

During major hatching peaks, otherwise cautious fish can be

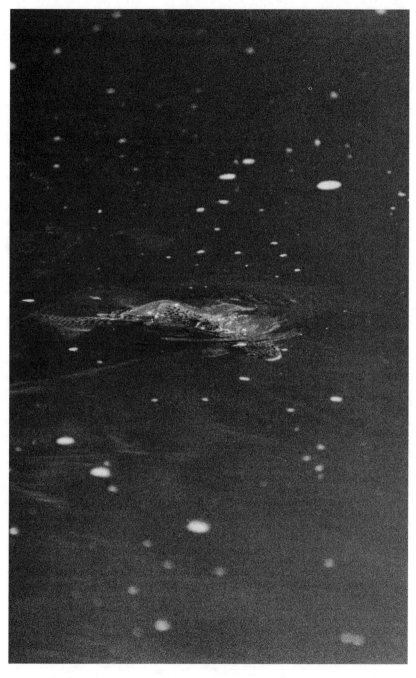

Spinners (dead flies) covering the surface of a stream provide nice meals for rainbow trout. An angler seeking a trout like this should "match the hatch" with the spinners.

Aquatic Insects   171

easy to catch. Fly fishermen often take and release limits. However, gamefish more often dine on a smorgasbord of aquatic larvae and pupae in simultaneously scattered hatches on streams and lakes. The most abundant hatch of insects, however, may not be the type or form of insect that fish favor.

At times, large numbers of smaller insects, such as caddis flies, compensate for their lack of bulk with hatch volume. This can be more appealing to savvy fish that are anxious to eat but want to expend little energy. At other times, subsurface pupae entice browsing bruisers while the obvious splashes on top belong to tiddlers. When you fish with aquatic insects and other baits, bring different types of baits so you can switch methods until you score.

In baiting with both the adult and larvae of the same species, it's critical to determine which bait form attracts the fish you see rising. Sometimes, you can use a dual rig and offer both the adult and larval form. An adult dobsonfly on a dropper above a casting bubble might complement a hellgrammite on a 3-foot-long leader below the bubble.

Though the larval insect stage (hellgrammites, for example) is the usual angler's choice, adult insects can be fished by using appropriate rigs; you aren't limited to nymphs. You will, of course, have to hatch or catch your own adults for bait, which is easily done during a hatch. Also, use very tiny wire hooks and light leaders.

When planning your fishing trips and bait selection, remember that hatches are keyed by air and water temperature—not by the date on the calendar. The date of the individual hatch can vary each year depending upon climate, rainfall and ambient temperatures. As already noted, it's the order in which hatches occur on a given stream or in a given area that is set. This is also true for "hot" fishing periods in most areas, so log the order during the year and check fishing reports.

Fly fishermen spend incredible amounts of time trying to determine what size and pattern of fly to fish where and when. More realistic bait anglers do well fishing bait as close as possible to the spot where it was collected. This can be as simple as netting bait right on the spot or as complex as setting up your own tanks at home and toting the baits back to their natal waters.

Adult Aquatic Bugs

Adult aquatic insects don't last very long; some mate and die

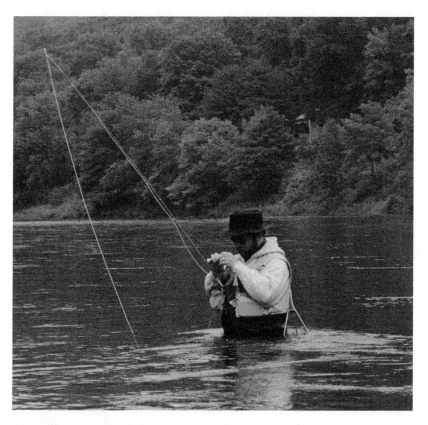

Bait anglers can take a cue from the persistent fly fisherman's painstaking efforts to "match the hatch." Check for apparent forage and make your adjustments accordingly.

the day they hatch. Others seem difficult to catch and nearly impossible to keep for long periods, so bait dealers often don't offer "adult aquatics." Fortunately, catching mayflies, dobsonflies, stoneflies and dragonflies can be as easy as waving a net at the water. A cheesecloth insert cut and sewn to fit your landing net works nicely. A big butterfly net with a long handle works even better. There's no mystery to it. Simply, "catch it, hook it and fish it."

It's possible to collect newly emerging insects with your hands after they hatch—before their wings dry and they zoom off. Because mayflies and caddis flies hatch in water, they can be nabbed with a small aquarium net as they float by. It's also not a bad tool to use when damselflies and dragonflies are hatching from shore or, for that matter, before grasshoppers dry their wings early on dewy mornings. You can use it to collect the adults for bait from the covered, semi-submerged holding tanks where your aquatic larvae are kept.

Nocturnal collecting works, too. For example, if you're staying overnight near water, it's easy to catch adult dobsonflies, along with terrestrials such as moths. If you hang a lamp at the end of a dock, you can literally "fish 'em where you find 'em." Trout, panfish and bass will gather to feast on bugs that suffer the misfortune of falling into the water.

Catching bait by hand quickly shows you that it's incredibly easy to mash these delicate insects. After you swoop down with a net on a likely flying bait, flip the net over the rim to close it. Hold an open container such as a baby food jar over the netted insect. Quickly pop the lid on the container after releasing the insect from the net. Hold the bait by the wings while hooking it.

Carrying Adult Aquatics

Small containers such as transparent film canisters can hold two or three adult insects for a short time. Transparent plastic containers are the best choice, because glass ones can break. Large containers don't work well because most of your bait flies out when they're opened. If you fish from a boat or don't mind a heavy creel, you can pack small containers of adult insects on ice or in cold water. This will slow the insects' metabolisms, making it easier to catch and handle them.

You can avoid the toting problem if you immediately bait up insects caught at the water, especially if there is enough of a hatch to draw decent-sized fish to the surface. If you mash a few, simply toss them in the water to create chum. Otherwise, larger gamefish won't bother with adult aquatic insects. This is because they use up more energy than they gain; fish don't diet by choice. They much prefer the easy life.

Buying Or Catching Aquatic Larvae

When anglers can't or won't catch their own, they can sometimes find hellgrammites, wigglers and, rarely, dragonfly nymphs at their local bait shops. Look for lively insects fresh from a water tank that's not carpeted with dead bugs. Pass on any baits that look soft or sluggish. If you provide your own container, use a white one so you can examine each bait for condition more easily.

Most popular baits are regional in nature. For example, you don't find wigglers for sale in much of the West. In areas where baits aren't available, you will need to catch your own if you want to maximize your choices. Even where commercial baits are available, baits fresh from the water work better. Collect bait in the lake you plan to fish or in its feeder streams; be sure you "match the hatch."

Collecting is easy. In still waters, winnowing weeds over a floating mesh screen will provide more bait than you can use in a week. Shovel mud near the shore into a screen, then slosh the screen in water to remove the dirt; you'll find plenty.

All sorts of spots produce aquatic insects. These include muddy beaver-dam bases and sheltered spots around fallen trees or backwater bottoms that collect silt. Turning over rocks in current also works, if you have quick hands or are handy with using an aquarium net.

In moving water, an easy way to collect insects is with a net made from a window-sized screen supported by a pair of old broomsticks. These nets work best if a downstream partner holds the net while you turn over rocks and other cover upstream on the drift line. Although cheesecloth nets will work, aluminum window mesh is a more durable choice.

Grabbing baits or netting baits with a small aquarium net after turning over rocks is a great way to collect aquatic insects and other baits such as Mad toms. This eliminates having to carry bait with you. (Hellgrammites, however, do have pinchers, so consider using an aquarium net to capture them in the water. Keep your fingers behind their middle and you won't get pinched.)

Preserving Your Aquatic Larvae Catch

A good way to keep aquatic larvae happy is in an aerated aquarium. A collection of aquatic insects can teach you a lot about what goes on underwater. Add a crayfish or two and some minnows, small panfish or a bass and you can see who eats what and when. Small trout are good, too, but keeping an aquarium cool enough for trout isn't easy.

Coolers, gallon glass jars or even buckets will hold aquatic insects if the containers are well-aerated and kept cool in the shade. One regular aquarium pump with the right fittings can aerate several insect, siren and minnow tanks. Such pumps work even inside a refrigerator. Either run the pump's power cord in through the rubber seal or leave the pump outside. Insert the clear plastic air line through a short section of metal tubing which is pushed through a cut in the door's rubber seal.

Field Expedients

Most insects can be stored for the day in damp leaves or sphagnum moss that's kept reasonably cool. You can also use a "base bucket," which contains your main supply. (This supply should have been previously iced down in a cooler.) You can replenish the bait supply in your belt holder, tobacco can or your boat's ready container from the base bucket, and the bait will stay in better condition longer.

A batch of small containers fits nicely into the shell loops of an old hunting vest. A few samples of each bait seems best, and don't overlook stashing a few aquatic larvae in a damp white sock.

Adult Mayflies And Wigglers

Although a size 14 Cahill may be the most popular fly in America, a live, adult mayfly that is carefully hooked through the head on a very light-wire No. 16, wide-gap, turned-up eye hook smells a lot better to trout and panfish than the most lovingly tied chicken hackle. Also, if it is carefully presented on a dropper loop above a casting bobber, it should stand up to a cast or two. Don't worry if your mayfly sinks; it will take fish at mid-depth and on the bottom, too.

Because mayflies hatch in water, it is a while before their new wings harden. During this period, it's fairly easy to net them on the wing.

Ice anglers and steelheaders rely heavily on mayfly larvae, called wigglers in the Midwest. Wigglers work great because they are abundant in streams with mud or silt bottoms! Mayflies are, without question, the most common aquatic insect on these Midwestern waters.

Concentrations may reach 500 nymphs per square foot in prime silt-bottom habitat. Even though many of these nymphs are safely buried, trout, perch and other species that ate wigglers when they were fry obviously find that wigglers offer a lot of calories at a minimal cost. Therefore, the lust for mayflies seems permanently implanted in most gamefish.

A green drake dun—a subadult mayfly—is shown here. The mayfly larvae—called wigglers in some areas—also are a highly effective bait.

Wigglers certainly classify as tender baits. They simply don't cast well. Some anglers get around this by mashing them into a paste which is used to "sweeten" lure and fly presentations. Others will use minimum-weighted downstream drift presentations and forgo casting. A few use gentle sidearm casts with a smooth release which generally keep wigglers on the hook.

Bobbers help suspend wigglers just off the bottom on long downstream drifts through slack-current pools. If you fish wigglers on bottom rigs, you will get no coverage because they disappear into the mud. Ice anglers, of course, avoid the casting problem entirely, and do well with a direct drop. This approach also works for boaters seeking perch off weedbeds. In most cases, wigglers that wiggle off the hook help chum the location.

A No. 14 or smaller hook with a wide gap and a turned-up eye is the wiggler-angler's choice. Salmon egg hooks work well. All wiggler rigs hook more fish if they are on 2-pound test or lighter leader!

The nymph should be hooked through the wing buds in the middle of the body for maximum durability. Even so, nymphs often are lost during the cast. Many fishermen will thread two, three or four wigglers at a time on the hook. Jamming on more than that number is counter-productive.

If your bait tank becomes crowded, make sure to keep the water fresh or circulating so the wigglers can continue to breathe through their belly gills. Aerators, oxygen pills and frequent water changes improve survival rates. Wigglers are available just about anywhere in the Upper Midwest. Just make sure the shop's tanks are well aerated.

Caddis Flies

Inch-long and smaller caddis flies look like bouncy little tents as they float down frisky streams and rushing rivers that usually run over rocks and gravel bottom. In the West, the size 12 Elk Hair Caddis replicates these insects that make up much of the insect hatch on popular rocky rivers. As a trout bait, caddis flies are quite delicate. For that reason, anglers prefer to use the caddisworm. Like mayflies, caddis flies can be collected with a small net or pinched off the water before their wings harden enabling them to fly. Caddis-fly presentations favor hooks in the No. 12 to No. 18 range to match size variations.

Caddisworms grovel to form a twig-and-gravel case that, in some habitats, can carpet the slack-water bottom around rocks and boulders. These are the easiest aquatic insect baits to collect—just pick them off the rocks! If you collect upstream from where you expect to fish, the encased caddisworms you inadvertently crush during your harvesting will work as a gamefish's hors d'oeuvre until you supply the main course.

You can fish encased caddises or—after carefully pinching off its pebble-and-twig cast—caddisworms. A single caddisworm on a hook works nicely; however, some anglers hook several worms onto a No. 10 hook.

Craneflies, Water Worms And Pupae

Unfortunately, craneflies' skinny legs and wings tend to break off no matter how carefully an angler handles them. You may get one drift or dap per cranefly in beaver ponds and slack-water areas in streams. Then it's time to try a fresh bait.

Water worms, also known as cranefly larvae, look like hairless, aquatic caterpillars. They don't stay on hooks very well because they are mushy like caterpillars, too. The most secure way

Dobsonfly And Caddis Fly Baits

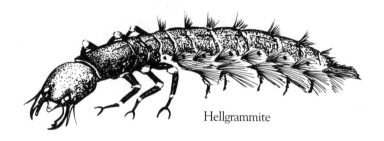

Hellgrammite

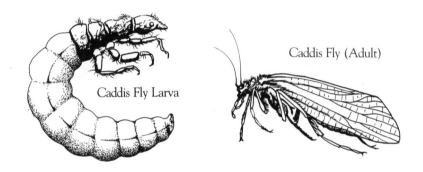

Caddis Fly Larva

Caddis Fly (Adult)

A hellgrammite (top), which is the larva of the dobsonfly, is a great bait for trout; the caddis fly larva (lower left) and, of course, the adult caddis fly (lower right) work, too.

to fish them is to wind them onto a long-shanked No. 8 hook with a wrap of self-adhesive, red-salmon-roe thread. The pupae stage offers a bit better "take" on a No. 6 or 8 hook. Both baits work the best when fished in slow-moving streams flowing between overgrown banks; however, neither would be a first-choice bait for most anglers.

Dobsonflies, Hellgrammites

Some of the larger dobsonfly species approach 6 inches in wingspan. Wing transparency and overall size are good field-identification marks. Most species work nicely in the pristine waters of alpine streams and glacial lakes for trout, smallmouth and panfish. A No. 6 or 8 hook inserted just above the wing base seems to work well.

Hellgrammites, dobsonfly larvae, are the favorite trout bait on Western streams and a dandy choice for river smallmouths and other species. A batch of different species can give the unwary handler a nasty nip with their conspicuous jaws which are used to catch, among other things, fish fry.

These dandy baits live under rocks and are so popular with fish in many larger streams that you have to turn over a lot of rocks to find a single bait. Check small tributary streams that can hold several dozen hellgrammites in each knee-deep pool. Most single-hook rigs that will bounce these baits along the bottom are good selections. Small bobbers work best over smooth bottoms. Pinch a tiny split shot 18 inches above the hook and drift the rig downstream along the stream's steep outer bank. In lakes, hellgrammites are most effective when worked around stream inlets.

Best of all, hellgrammites will keep several days in damp moss and are durable enough to stay on the hook for several catches.

Dragonflies And Larvae

Dragonflies catch trout in slower stream sections, beaver ponds and pools. They also work on smallmouth bass and other species when fished over weedbeds and along grassy banks.

Their double wings, extended at rest, are good field marks for these flying "darning needles" that favor slack water. Because of their antics and activity, they are a fine surface bait that will pull in fish from long distances on calm days. You'd expect these big flies to attract big fish, but this is not the case.

The dragonfly's larvae fall into the screen mesh of those who sort mud along banks of slow-moving streams. They vary widely in size, shape and color and are often confused with damselflies. They make good chum for those who prefer to bait with more durable larvae.

Damselflies And Their Larvae

Damselflies look like dragonflies, but hold their wings like salmon flies. Damselfly wings are transparent, too. Often confused with dragonflies, these baits are marginal because they aren't durable enough for slow-moving waters where they work best. They do make good chum and mix well with dragonflies in setting up artificial hatches. Whack them with a fly swatter to create your own instant chum slick or hatch.

"Wimpy dragonflies" best describes these wispy larvae that don't stay on hooks well. These can be mixed with mud and pitched by hand or shot with a sling shot into slow current to chum fish from downstream in areas where chumming is legal. Only the patient and near-sighted use these fragile baits.

Sowbugs

Aquatic sowbugs look like the terrestrial version known as the pill, or potato, bug. In some slack waters, especially alkaline rivers and less common lakes, sowbug numbers reach Manhattan population densities, tempting trout and other smaller gamefish.

It's easy to collect aquatic sowbugs while sorting through aquatic vegetation that also holds snails and insect larvae. In a pinch, terrestrial sowbugs can be substituted. Hook them on very small, light-wire hooks.

Stoneflies, Nymphs

Stoneflies inhabit rocky rivers and, in most cases, fast flowing streams. Their long, flat-to-the-body, mottled wings and long feelers are good field marks. Colors run to the dull side. These sturdy insects last for a longer period of time if kept in loosely rolled nylon stockings.

Most rivers—even slow ones—will be home to at least three or four species of stoneflies. In fast, rock-strewn rivers, there might be as many as 20 species. Even more important, stoneflies are pretty big as far as aquatic insects go. When their hatches rev up or their nymphs start moving about, it's action time for trout and smallmouth anglers. Salmon flies, which are the largest stoneflies, are extremely good baits for very large trout because their incredible hatches draw big fish up to the top. However, in many waters, it's the more numerous winter blacks that provide the most consistent action. Where winter stream-fishing is legal, it's possible to have stonefly hatches during any month.

Stonefly nymphs, characterized by their twin tails, stay moderately active even in extremely cold water. Salmon-fly nymphs are large enough to get most of the attention. However, the inch-long, dark, winter stoneflies can produce action in colder waters when nothing else stirs—if it's abundant and the bait of choice.

=15=

Terrestrial Insects

Accidents happen, and bugs fall into the water. Small bugs can float, buoyed by surface tension; big bugs can sink. All terrestrials, however, object violently to their unhappy introduction to the aquatic world. This "violent" action signals to gamefish that dinner's served. As a result, "terrestrials" work for fly fishermen if they imitate crickets, grasshoppers, cockroaches, caterpillars, cicadas, wasps, bees and hornets. Many other flying and crawling insects work, too. Big beetles, centipedes and a host of other insects deserve a try. Terrestrial insect larvae, which are popular baits with ice fishermen, work so well and come in so many flavors that the next chapter is devoted entirely to them.

The number of terrestrial insects presented to gamefish is much smaller than that of aquatic insects. In theory, they should be less effective; however, they are not. Why? Terrestrials in water are an easy meal because, like fish out of water, they are out of their element. Because terrestrials blow or drop into the water at rather odd and unannounced intervals, they attract fish even when there is not a hatch. Terrestrials, at least those commonly used as bait, are fairly large, too. The result for anglers is two effective commercially available baits, grasshoppers and crickets, as well as some alternatives.

Clearly naturals cost less and work better than fancy flies or plastic, scent-impregnated imitations. However, choices are limited in many parts of the country. Crickets appear to be the most

Even though crickets are used often as bait, they can be difficult to handle and get on a hook. Keeping them cool and semi-dormant before use is the key.

popular commercial insect bait. Grasshoppers are sometimes available, and the catalpa worm is a successful bream (bluegill) bait in the South. Aside from that, "what you catch is what you get." By taking the time to catch your own baits, you will enjoy a secret weapon for taking species such as trout, bass and panfish.

Every 15 to 30 seconds, toss a cricket or caterpillar into a stream and a big, bottom-hugging brown trout or smallmouth may be convinced that it's time for dinner on top. From a lake's meadow bank, flip grasshoppers up into an offshore wind and, as the hoppers blow out over deeper water, you'll see them disappear into the mouths of hungry fish that almost always are cruising within casting range.

Years ago, crickets were the extent of the commercial insect baits. Today, you can buy a variety of crickets and grubs from various bait sellers. The smell of the establishment will tell you the quality of the bait offered. If the seller's stock containers are available for inspection, see if they're carpeted with dead insects. Be aware of the ambient temperature in the bait storage areas.

Crickets should be lively, and their storage container should be cool and moist. Caterpillars, as well as grasshoppers, do best if kept in their natural habitat food material—tree leaves or grass, for example.

Collecting And Keeping Insects

Because there are so many different kinds of insects, catching them requires varied techniques. For those who use bees, wasps and hornets, a dash of heroism or, without proper techniques, an absence of good sense is needed. A basic bug catcher's outfit would include a fine-mesh butterfly net, traps made from coffee cans and a wool blanket which can be placed under vegetation to trap bugs shaken off the leaves. Fly swatters will stun flying bugs, and other items, such as hollow-bread cricket traps, also work.

Spending an evening on the porch near a screen door or yard light is the best method. The number, size and variety of insects you can net or swat is incredible. Don't be afraid to experiment with different insects as bait because nobody knows what might work in your area until you try! Contact neighborhood organic gardeners who would appreciate someone removing critters that are munching on their produce. For example, cutworms that rank among the top garden pests make marvelous bait! (Special methods for catching popular baits will be covered in their individual sections.)

Insects with stingers, such as wasps, mud daubers and bees, work nicely as bait. Of course, you need to treat adults with great care—handle them with gloves and tweezers. One thing is certain: Not many anglers use them for bait; however, they work because their imitations, like the well-known McGinty fly, work. For the more conservative angler or those who want to bottom fish, the larvae of these insects work even better.

Most insects keep well in a cool, shaded spot. Screen-topped boxes work nicely as containers for terrestrials. Bigger is better with these boxes as long as you have a way of removing small quantities of bait without causing a general jail break. A "vestibule arrangement" featuring a small secondary area that you can

As the author notes, a woman's nylon stocking makes a good carrying case for crickets. If they're kept cool, you should be able to remove one from the stocking without losing the entire batch.

cut off from the main container works well. A scrap aluminum window screen with only the support of a simple frame works.

Food and water needs vary by species. Don't overfeed. As a rule, insects do better with minimal fresh food. Decayed food and dead or dying insects should be promptly removed so that the remaining insects remain healthier and happier longer.

Toting Insects

Anyone who has ever tried to get a cricket or grasshopper out of a bait container knows there must be a better way. All sorts of commercial containers work. Some rotate while others use little chutes to guide bait to within grasping range.

Women's knee-high stockings—new or used—make super bug holders. The trick is to cool down the bugs in the refrigerator or collect the bait from the stock box in the cool night air. Put about a dozen crickets or grasshoppers in a stocking foot, shake it down and tie the top off with a rubber band. The loosely rolled stocking can be carried in a vest pocket, a creel or cooler. Even damp leaves will work. When you need bait, it's easy to pick the right stocking, especially if you color-code stockings for crickets, hoppers or whatever. When you open the top, the stocking's weave will secure the dormant bait so you can hook up.

Care And Use Of Crickets

Many fishing experts consider using crickets as bait to be rather overrated. Crickets are popular with commercial growers because they are easy to grow. However, crickets are so delicate as bait that they require the finest wire hooks, and they don't last long. They are, however, effective as a panfish bait. Although there are a number of species, most store-bought types are the large, black field crickets that, like grasshoppers, reach peak size and numbers just before the first freeze in the fall.

Catching crickets is easy. Most species will wander into traps made from hollowed bread or coffee cans which are baited with bread and sugar and left out overnight. Picking crickets up and putting them in a bait container can be another story, however. Some use cardboard scoops to grab crickets. (One imaginative type uses a cordless vacuum cleaner to collect crickets which he then dumps into holding cans.) Flooding a good cricket habitat (Crickets don't like water.) forces them out to where you can catch them.

Crickets can be hooked through the back on a No. 8 or 10 fine-wire hook. Hooks with fine wire soldered to the shank allow the cricket to be tied to the shank. Tiny rubber bands used by orthodontists and self-adhesive thread used for spawn-bag fishing also deserve a try.

Raising crickets isn't difficult, either. A large container, such as a standard-sized garbage can, is basic. Cover the top with a wire screen. Plastic containers may be slick enough to keep crickets from climbing out; otherwise, coat the top 10 inches or so of the inside of the container with a spray-on wax or polish so crickets can't climb out. Put a 6-inch layer of damp sand in the bottom, covering the sand with straw. Add about 24 crickets. You can, if you like, sex crickets by the terminal tube on the tail; half of each

Casting Bubble And Cricket Rig

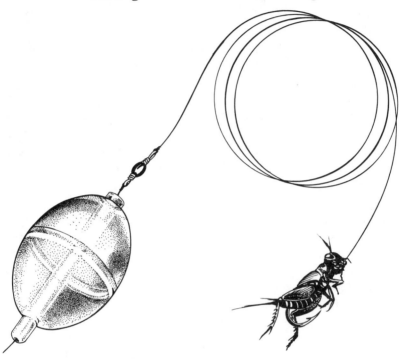

A No. 8, light-wire hook is about the right size for hooking crickets. The hook can be threaded through the body. A casting bubble helps put the bait where you want it.

sex is ideal. Food is provided in a small container of poultry mash, and water is poured onto a saucer layered with cotton so the young crickets won't drown. As an alternative, a small screened container of crickets can be placed in a warm, dry spot like on top of the water heater. If you plan to grow crickets year-round, you will need warmth—growth slows during winter. At 80 degrees, it takes crickets about three months to mature; at 60 degrees, it takes much longer. An aquarium or terrarium heater or a light bulb hung in the container can provide enough heat for year-round production.

Gourmet Grasshoppers

Few baits can beat grasshoppers for tempting gamefish into topwater action. Whether it's big black or brown spotted grasshoppers from the ground or little yellow or green leaf hoppers from plants, all sorts of hoppers produce if properly presented as top-water or mid-depth baits for tempting trout and bass.

Catching grasshoppers can be as easy as a trip to a meadow or other grassy area just after sunrise on a dewy morning. Grasshoppers can't fly well until their wings dry and, like all insects, they are much less active in cooler temperatures. This is the best time to stun them with a light whack of a fly swatter and put them in a container until needed. Athletic types may try to catch hoppers on the fly with a butterfly net. It's also possible to catch grasshoppers by driving them into ditches or holes that are deeper than they are wide—grasshoppers can't hop out of them.

Toting hoppers on a stream or lake can be a problem for those who don't want to pocket a stocking roll of active grasshoppers. All sorts of commercial contraptions are sold, and they work—sometimes. Anyone who has opened a container of previously cool, dormant grasshoppers in the heat of the day knows how they got their name. A few hoppers can be carried in film canisters punched full of holes. Having only one or two hoppers per container helps you avoid mass escapes. Smaller hoppers can be carried in cricket holders. A piece of Velcro put inside the container's lid will usually hold the hopper's legs long enough for you to get your hook set. In your boat, hopper containers should be kept on ice in the cooler so the hoppers stay calm until hooked.

Grasshoppers can be driven into streams or lakes to create an instant hatch, too. This works best when the wind is blowing in the right direction across meadow areas, allowing you to drive hoppers downwind. The windward side of the lake is, of course, the best spot to fish any flying terrestrial, because that's where the insects naturally appear. Trout, in particular, are suckers for hoppers along a meadowed shore. Where alpine winds, for example, regularly come up every afternoon, blowing across a meadow onto a lake, fish will cruise in and wait. In situations like this, consider dapping.

The easiest approach in hooking hoppers is to simply hook them lightly under the collar with a light-wire, long-shank hook—No. 10 to No. 16 seem typical—in one of several configurations. For example, the insect can be threaded onto the hook so that the bend is flush with the head or tail. Grasshoppers attached to special hooks with ultra-thin wire or a tie with thread or

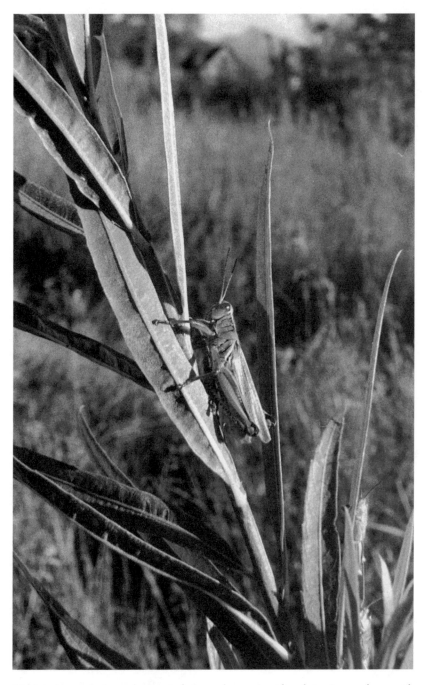

The best time to catch grasshoppers is during early morning when their wings are heavy with dew, which prevents them from flying. Then, like this one, they are easily netted.

Terrestrial Insects 189

rubber bands keep hoppers livelier longer. If your hopper doesn't float, use a lighter wire or smaller-sized hook.

If possible, add nothing to the rig. Float hoppers downcurrent along the bank or use a long rod to dance hoppers on the water's surface. Try to stay low, though, so the fish don't spot you. If more casting weight is needed, tie a comfortable-weight casting bubble to the end of the line and place a 4- or 5-foot-long leader above the hooked hopper.

Most anglers switch to crickets when they're fishing deep; however, hoppers can work there, too. A standard split-shot rig will sink hoppers down to the realm of big brown trout or bass holding deep in streams and rivers. This setup also works around inlet creeks during the dead days of summer when fish are lethargic. A light weight on the hopper rig allows you to use the current of an inlet stream to move the bait naturally into the lake or reservoir. Submerging the rodtip helps put the bait beneath shallow surface currents into the deeper holes where the big fish lie in wait for easy meals.

Hoppers aren't a real sturdy bait, and can be tough to find if you don't raise them yourself. That's why commercially prepared hoppers—both preserved in liquid or freeze-dried—can save the day. You can, as with crickets, freeze your own casualties for later use, too.

Cockroaches As Bait

Some say that in Florida, anglers just put a leash on a cockroach and won't let it out of the water until it comes up with a big bass. Granted, cockroaches are unlovely critters to look at, but they seem to be a particularly good panfish and trout bait if carefully threaded onto a hook like a cricket. As most people know, cockroaches are alpine-type climbers. If you put a stick upright in the middle of a large container, you'll find an inhabitant of your roach motel sitting on top of the stick every time you open the lid.

Butterflies And Moths

If you let those caterpillars munch on leaves too long, the next time you open your storage box you can watch a cloud of butterflies or moths wing off into the sunset. Even though moths and butterflies aren't commonly used by anglers, fly specialists know the advantages of patterns that imitate butterflies. In the West, a

Other Insect Baits

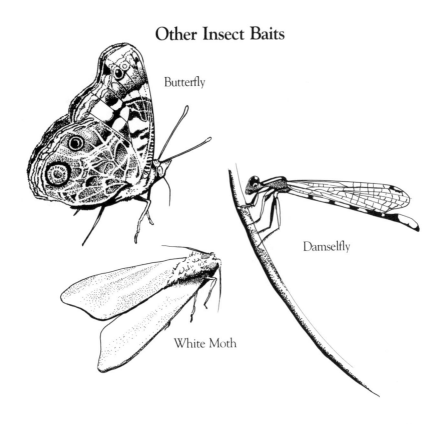

Butterfly

Damselfly

White Moth

A common butterfly (upper left), a damselfly (right) or even a white moth work well as bait when fish are going after insects. All can be found at most fishing locations.

host of spruce moths tempt trout; however, some of the bigger butterflies, such as Monarchs, seem too large for most fish. They also taste awful, which is the reason birds won't eat them.

However, most other moth and butterfly species work well. In the West, for example, spruce and other conifer moths live in drought-damaged forests in huge numbers. When quite substantial numbers arrive at one time, such as during the migration of certain butterfly species, it amounts essentially to a terrestrial "hatch." Just make sure you're not using an endangered species!

It's possible to raise both butterflies and moths, given the proper larvae and conditions. However, it's easier to see these as "targets of opportunity" in the field. If you take along a mesh insert that fits into your favorite landing net, you will have the proper tool for collecting these baits—once you see fish taking them.

Ways Of Hooking Grasshoppers

Grasshoppers can be hooked several ways. They can be hooked under the collar or the hook can be threaded through the body so that the point protrudes from the tail or near the collar.

Both baits work best when, like grasshoppers, they flutter on top; therefore, use a light hook pushed through the body. A long rod or pole and the proper use of a trailing wind (to move your bait over holes in weedbeds or along the edge of undercut banks) improves results.

Beetle Mania?

Beetles come in hundreds of species and sizes, ranging from the tiny borers to the Western hummingbird beetles that are as big as birds. Like bumblebees, beetles don't always look like they can fly. Many beetles will sink; a few will float. Most beetles, however, catch fish if presented like crickets. Experiment!

You can collect beetles and their larvae by lifting the bark on dead, downed trees and stumps; raking decaying organic matter (duff), piles of leaves and garden compost; and poking around a number of other dark, damp and downright unattractive—unless you are a beetle—locations. They tote like crickets and, in the case of some of the big staghorns, take large fish. Some beetles will bite, so use hemostats.

Cicadas: Long Awaited Bait

Seventeen years is a long time to wait for bait; however, if you hit the 17-year cycle right, you'll find that fish will welcome these locusts which are best hooked with a thin-wire hook and fished on top. If you don't hit the cycle's peak, you can still find these baits; it just takes more time and listening per bait. You will discover that the male cicadas are rather loud. However, they are difficult to find and grab, so consider using a net!

The Ultimate Bug

With the possible exception of moths with 10-inch wingspans from the Philippines, the ultimate bug bait may be living in New Guinea. Locals fish the Eurcanthra lato, a big beetle, without using hooks. A thread is tied to its thorny leg; it acts as its own hook and bait. It seems likely that these beetles will eventually be offered as bait in the United States.

=====16=====

Terrestrial Larvae

Terrestrial larvae, in theory, should not work as well for bait as aquatic insects which are available in greater numbers on a day-to-day basis. So why devote a chapter to these baits? Terrestrial larvae, which have long been the top bait for those who fish through the ice, have, with the introduction of more sophisticated European bait-fishing techniques and increased interest in very light gear, spread to other venues and species. When fishing conditions get tough, terrestrial larvae take fish!

Perhaps the reason for this is they are totally defenseless. No other live bait looks as safe to eat and easy to gobble as a terrestrial larva. It's clear why these are the fastest growing segment of the bait market. Nothing else is so easy to buy, catch, keep, carry and use. However, they do require special and, usually, delicate rigs and careful handling for the best results.

Grubbing Grubs

Grubs which are the larval stage of land insects come in more flavors than popular brands of ice creams. Mealworms, corn grubs, goldenrod grubs, stump or white grubs and a squirming collection of others offer enough bait options to tempt the most picky trout, panfish or bass. Most grubs keep well in the refrigerator or in cool areas, such as root cellars. Most species seem easy to hold all winter. You can also freeze grubs, although this will soften them considerably.

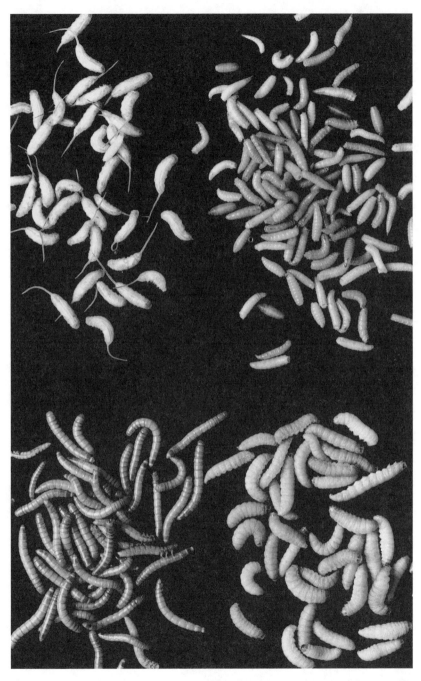

Live larvae baits are good choices, particularly for smaller gamefish such as panfish. Clockwise from upper left are mousies, Eurolarvae, golden grubs (mealworms) and waxworms.

Terrestrial Larvae

Some species, like mealworms, are available at bait and pet shops. Others, such as goldenrod or acorn grubs, are easy to collect all winter long by anyone with enough of a botanist's eye to tell an oak from an elm and a goldenrod from a thistle. However, you may have trouble beating birds to the bait.

Growing grubs requires a growth medium, like grain, and enough containers to separate the adults, bait larvae and intermediate pupae stages. A kitchen sieve helps in sorting the forms. Picky types may want to use gloves when working with maggots; nose clips and surgical masks are optional. Acorn and goldenrod grubs smell better and are easier to glean.

Mealworms As Bait

Black darkling beetles that ruin flour in the kitchen and grains in feed elevators produce mealworms—striped tan and golden grubs. If you can't buy them, just pick over spilled grains at the local grain elevator or feed store. You should be able to find both the beetle and the mealworm.

Mealworms are so small that you need to use tiny thin-wire, fly-type hooks even when putting several on at a time. You may need a lot of this bait to get you through a day or the season!

Fortunately, once you obtain a few dozen mealworms, locate a couple 2- to 4-quart containers and add a little bran or chicken mash with some flour, you can be guaranteed a constant supply. Simply put mealworms in a bucket filled about halfway with grain, bran or chicken mash and toss in a wet napkin each day so the growing medium stays moist. The napkins will hold pupae until they hatch into darkling beetles.

Then, use your sieve or a slotted spoon to move the adult darkling beetles to a second container full of flour where they can lay eggs. These eggs will hatch and produce mealworms in four to six weeks. Sieve the flour to separate out the mealies, leaving the adult beetles. Carry the mealies to the water in a container filled about halfway with wood shavings. You're now set for the season!

Goldenrod And Acorn Grubs

These are two dandy, if rather small and sometimes delicate, baits that live in goldenrod stems and acorns, respectively. Both are about the size of popcorn and both store best refrigerated in their natal goldenrod galls or acorns.

Acorn, Goldenrod Grubs

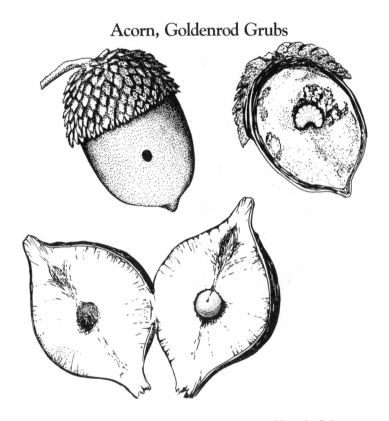

A hole in an acorn (top) reveals the presence of grub; a hole in a goldenrod gall (bottom) means the grub is gone. Both grubs, although small, make a good bait, particularly for panfish.

Goldenrod grubs, the larvae of the goldenrod gall fly, collect easily from fall to spring when other baits are difficult to find. Goldenrod plants with the swollen galls on their stems can be found in meadows and along the edges of woods lining streams in the lowlands. As a rule, you can collect grubs for years from the same patch if you leave some galls for restocking.

Carefully examine each swollen gall. Tiny holes indicate that the grubs have left home; fairly large holes mean a bird beat you to your bait. In either case, the gall isn't worth harvesting. The "unholy" galls should be nipped off and saved in a refrigerator until needed. Then, very carefully, slit each gall open and remove the grub. (Use the collected grubs immediately or store them in grain in the refrigerator.)

Acorn grubs are the larvae of acorn weevils; other species of

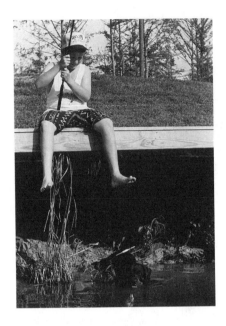

Stump grubs are part of the beetle cycle. The beetles are found in the rotten wood of decaying stumps or fallen timber. These grubs are good bait for trout, smallmouths and larger panfish.

nut weevil larvae live in pecans, walnuts and other nuts. To be sure that fallen acorns contain grubs, look for a tiny hole in acorns and other nuts. These baits seem to be interchangeable with goldenrod grubs.

White Or Stump Grubs

These nice-sized baits come from beetles—scarab and others—that live in rotten wood of stumps or fallen timber. Most grubs are white or tan with a dark head—a good, tough spot to insert a small, sharp hook. All keep well in whatever medium you find them in originally. Just add potato slices or damp napkins so the medium stays moist—not wet—and never dries out. Decomposed bark works particularly well.

Stump grubs rank with hellgrammites as trout baits. They tempt smallmouths when nothing else will, and they are a dandy bait for larger panfish. In many parts of the West, stump grubs are the top bait for rainbow and cutthroat trout. Nothing could be easier to gather when you run out of bait on the stream!

Corn Borers

These mini-worms work well under the ice for all sorts of panfish. They are so tough that it's not unusual to take more than one fish with a single bait. You can buy these in some bait shops or collect them from corn into which they have bored. Most farmers who raise corn spray pesticides to control these worms, so don't overlook local gardeners as a source. Cobs with borer holes and borers can be kept refrigerated in a closed container for weeks or, if you prefer, carefully cut borers out of the cobs and store them throughout the winter refrigerated in a covered container partially filled with cornmeal.

However, corn borers can be a pain to keep while you're ice fishing. The solution, however, is simple: Cut corrugated cardboard into strips as wide as your bait container. Wind the strips into a coil in the jar and dump in the borers. They will move down along the corrugations and, if stored in the refrigerator, go dormant. Then, tear off a strip of cardboard just before you head out to fish. The cardboard can be wrapped in a plastic bag and stashed in a pocket until needed.

Maggots, Eurolarvae And Mousies

Silver wigglers or "spikes" are the socially acceptable names for maggots which are all too easily identified because of their enchanting smell. Housefly, stable-fly and blowfly maggots are the most usual types. These mini-maggots are only a half-inch in length; several of them can be threaded onto a hook at one time, or they can be used to sweeten even the smallest ice-fishing baits. They work well for panfish and even trout. However, the larger Eurolarvae that come in attractive colors seem to be the choice.

Fly names suggest maggot acquisition methods. Blowflies and houseflies will lay their eggs on a piece of rotting meat hung in an out-of-the-way spot. Stable flies, as you might expect, lay their eggs in manure. From four days to a week later, the fly eggs hatch into maggots. The maggots can be shook or tapped off into a container filled with stale cornflakes or bran for use or storage. A small amount of commercial fish attractant or anise oil mixed in with the meal or bran improves the smell. A couple teaspoons of oil mixed to a quart container of bran does the job. Add food dye to the storage medium to dye your own maggots. Red, orange, blue and green seem to be favorite colors. Start with a tablespoon of dye, which is available from a craft shop; add more after a couple of weeks if your maggots aren't colorful enough. You can, of course, dye and scent store-bought maggots, too.

This messy task is done for you when you buy Eurolarvae, the commercially available maggots that seem so popular with ice anglers. These are grubs of choice for most panfish, trout and other small gamefish species because they are larger, more colorful and usually better conditioned than "regular" maggots.

Mousies

Ice anglers wouldn't make it through the season without their mousies—rat-tailed maggots. To the casual observer, mousies might seem to belong in the aquatic insect section because they live in water and breath air through a long, tail-like snorkle tube connected to the head.

Given winter prices, most anglers collect mousies in cheesecloth nets around the outflows of the local cannery or in extremely wet cow manure at the dairy farm or feedlot.

Keeping mousies is as easy as putting them in a small container filled with wood shavings—not plywood or pressed wood—and stashing it in a cool spot until needed.

Bee, Sawfly And Other Interesting Larvae

Heroes can fish with live or recently deceased stinging insects. Wasp larvae, for example, can be collected from hanging nests after dark or with the aid of insect spray or a smoker—all fairly risky. However, wasp, hornet, yellow jacket and bee larvae are widely available as a dead byproduct of hearth-and-home insect control, so see your local pest control company. Such insects make great chum if properly rinsed so insecticides don't end up in the stream. Live or dead larvae fished with this kind of chum take fish! If they are alive, however, they seem to require more effort and risk than their performance deserves.

Elm sawfly larvae do seem to be an exception to the above rule. These big baits—some run to 1½ inches in length—shake out of elm and willow trees in spring and summer. Any grub with a dark stripe down its back that falls onto cheesecloth (or an old sheet) spread out under a tree deserves a try. Most vary from light green to yellow, but similar larvae in tan and even orange also work. Think in technicolor!

Waxworms

Beekeepers can supply you with waxworms and beeswax to

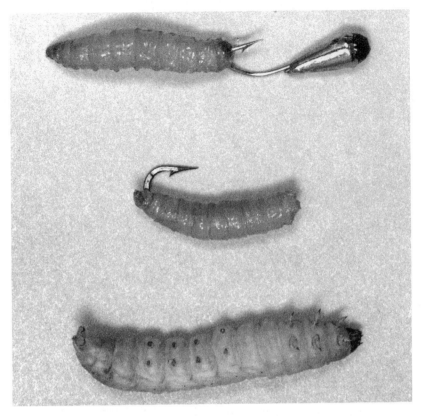

Waxworms are a popular bait that you can easily grow. Collect or buy some and then start producing them. If you don't let the moths escape, you should have a continual bait supply.

help you begin raising your own supply. Waxworms are the larvae of moths. These moths lay their eggs in beehives so their larvae can live off the wax. This is not popular with beekeepers, so use them as a source to provide information or direction to old, abandoned hives typically infested with these pests.

If you collect or buy waxworms in the spring and summer, you can raise them all year. The growth medium should be similar to a beehive. Mix a one-pound box of cornflakes, ½ cup honey, ½ cup Karo syrup and ½ cup water in a mesh-covered gallon-sized glass jar or plastic container. Add about a dozen or so grubs, and cover the container.

The grubs will eventually come to the surface to spin cocoons. At this time, add a piece of corrugated cardboard. When the moths hatch, they will lay their eggs on it. You can use this card-

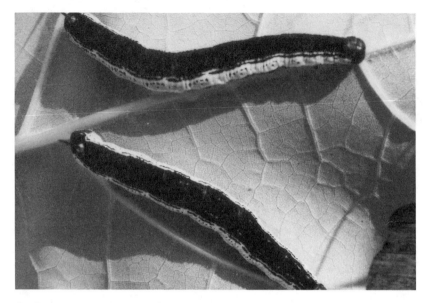

Catalpa worms are a favorite in the South for catching spring panfish. Anglers who are in the know often cut the end off and with a matchstick turn the worm inside out so its fluids will attract fish.

board to start another jar; however, take care not to let the moths escape.

Caterpillars, Catalpas And Webworms

Any gardener knows that caterpillars and other crawling critters that form pupae and hatch into butterflies or moths come in a host of varieties. Most will work as bait. Cutworms, tomato worms and several others are probably in your garden.

Fuzzy critters' sizes and colors vary widely. Inchworms are so small that they can barely squeeze onto a No. 18 hook. Some caterpillars, like hornworms, are large enough to tempt a big largemouth or supply two baits for smaller fish. Regional favorites usually escape national notice. In the South, the catalpa worm with its black stripes on its back remains a local favorite for spring panfish. Tent caterpillars, corn earworms and anything else big enough to slip onto a hook works, too.

Rigging caterpillars is easy on any of the usual garden-worm or nightcrawler setups. Several can be threaded onto the same hook. However, the "inside-out" method often used with catalpa worms seems to work best for those who do not mind the mess. First, cut

Terrestrial Larvae

off the caterpillar's head; then using a toothpick or twig stuck into the uncut end, push the caterpillar inside out. Usually, an appropriate-sized hook—No. 6 to No. 8, depending upon the caterpillar—is hooked through the middle. An even better method uses a smaller, long-shanked No. 10 to No. 14 hook. This enables you to thread on the bait so the hook's bend barely extends past the cut end of the caterpillar.

If you collect caterpillars, catalpa worms and the like near where you are fishing, try to fish under, or at least near, similarly related vegetation. Panfish and bass commonly hang out under catalpa trees, waiting for worms unfortunate enough to fall into the water.

All caterpillars are easy to maintain in a mesh-covered container if you take the time to collect leaves from their host plants. Add fresh leaves—or even lettuce—once or twice a week. Some species, like catalpa worms, are quite "species specific" in their food requirements; others eat almost anything. Most will die if they eat leaves coated with garden insect spray. If you want to slow the life cycle so your baits don't spin cocoons, place the containers in the refrigerator.

=17=

Insect, Larvae Presentations

I nsects and larvae, by their size and generally delicate nature, require much lighter gear than most anglers are accustomed to using. Two- or 4-pound-test line, hooks from No. 8 on down and matching bobbers, shot and other terminal tackle make these baits a fine choice for savvy anglers who want to put more sport into their fishing. Trout, panfish and other modest-sized fish can still challenge tackle and technique. It's important to understand that bait is bait. Most insect and larvae presentations also work with worms, small minnows and leeches.

As always, these presentations divide into still- and moving-water types. Separating topwater, mid-depth and bottom approaches helps you see what works best in different situations. Of course, there will be overlapping here, too. Because this is the least developed form of American bait fishing, major discoveries are yet to be made. Experiment!

Matching baits and habitats works best. Grasshoppers suit meadow streams. Caddis flies and their cases work over mud bottoms or in slow-moving waters that hold these baits; stoneflies favor faster water. Watch where the naturals lurk, catch some and fish them just downstream.

Still-Water Insects And Larvae

Motion, caused from the bait or the retrieve, keys the action in still water. Moving baits increase the sphere of discovery and offer more intensive coverage. Currents can't draw fish to your

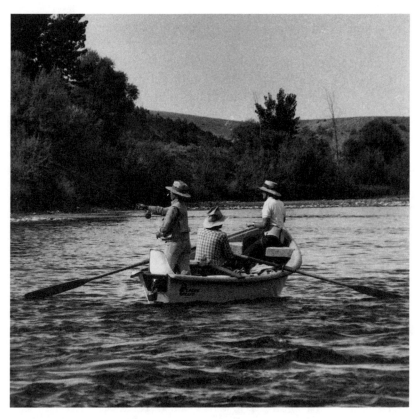

These anglers allow their boat to drift as they work floating insects along the shoreline. In this situation, the oars help slow the boat's drift and keep it parallel to the bank.

bait, so you must move the bait to the fish. A few larvae, like the dragonfly's, swim with jet propulsion in short puffs—not too much movement, though!

Insects offer more subtle movements than a crayfish's dash or a minnow's dart. You will need to help things along with judicious reeling and constant attention.

Grasshoppers and big aquatic insects that "buzz" on the surface deserve top billing. A long pole—even 20 feet isn't excessive—with about 6 feet of line and a hooked hopper fished in a big bed of weeds or lily pads among some cooperative panfish or bass produces. This approach also works with dragonflies—hook two on one hook. Lazy boaters can wind-drift using a floating insect and, to keep line from sinking it, a bobber. Power upwind along the shore while trolling a minnow; then drift back towing a topwater bait that adds variety to your presentation.

Even with ultra-light gear, an unweighted bait won't cast far. You need to add a terminal casting bubble and a dropper farther up toward the rodtip. This is the standard topwater rig for still water because as you retrieve, the bait meets the fish before the bubble arrives. You can also run a leader behind the casting bubble to give fish a choice of baits.

Many aquatic insects swim to the surface, pause and hatch in the film. Until their wings dry, these insects are incredibly vulnerable to fish, birds and other hungry critters. Presenting such baits in the surface film is possible with the standard topwater rig. You can also use any other float with casting weight, several feet of leader (preferably dressed with fly floatant) and, of course, a light-wire hook.

Mid-Depth Presentations

The most natural sinking bait presentation can't be too slow. Use a wire-stem bobber with enough shot crimped on the stem to sink the bobber to its mark. Add up to 4 feet of leader (unless fishing the shallows), a light-wire hook and the bait.

Feather your line during the cast to avoid slack. Count to five, close the bail and wait out the drop for a couple of minutes. Then retrieve and cast again. You will get a faster drop with a ring or center slider above a big insect or larva and just enough shot to take the bait to the bottom. Cast to a spot and leave the bail open until the bait stops dropping.

With a larger bobber and more weight, you can reverse this method to present insects "on the rise." Cast to the spot and let your bait sink. Be prepared for a hit on the drop, even though it doesn't happen very often. When the line stops, start a slow retrieve—a foot or two a minute is fast enough for baits swimming up to the surface to hatch. You need a big bobber that will stay put while you are reeling in. This system works particularly well when caddis flies are hatching. To exactly duplicate their movement, continue reeling in slowly until your bait is about a foot below the surface, then increase the speed of your retrieve. When the type of aquatic insect is known and evening hatches are consistent, you will take fish before the surface action begins.

Mid-depth insects include various swimming aquatic types, such as dobson- and dragonflies. You should fish these insects

This largemouth bass was taken by the author on a dragonfly that was dapped over the edge of the bullrushes. Don't overlook bait that may exist all around you—the fish won't.

where they are naturally found with the standard graduated shot system under a bobber with the smallest diameter possible. Caddis, for example, would be fished over mud bottom; stoneflies, over gravel or rocks. Dragonflies and dobsonflies that live on larvae and other nymphs prefer a more open bottom than do most other species because they can find meals more easily.

Use a fixed bobber and retrieve at the speed that your bait of choice would achieve on its own. This can be about hull speed when you wind-drift in a boat or canoe. If the wind is blowing too hard, clamp paddles or oars to the gunwale (with c-clamps) at right angles to your destination and you will slow down. By making adjustments in the way in which the oars are clamped (for example, clamping one oar at an angle smaller than 90 degrees), you can even drift at an angle to the wind, rather than with the wind.

Insect, Larvae Presentations   207

Back On The Bottom

Presenting insects on or just off the bottom instead of hiding them among the bottom hazards (where the hemisphere of discovery shrinks to the size of a lemon) keys the action. Fixed float systems work best in up to rod-length-deep water with graduated shot rigs being the choice. Windbeater rigs combined with baits like hellgrammites or water worms work in heavily fished waters where fish cautiously pick up baits and drop them if they feel the least resistance. Sliding sinker fish-finder rigs, especially if used with mini-marshmallows (to provide flotation for the insect), do the job, too.

Traditional double-dropper setups with two larvae or a larva and an aquatic insect work nicely. You can, if you fish from a boat or steep bank, pick the sinker up; then set it down. This disturbs the bottom, causing larvae to emerge from the mud. This slow, non-threatening movement attracts fish from a considerable distance in clear water. In heavily fished waters, delicate ice-fishing systems with tiny lures and baits seem to take fish when no other method works.

Bank and boat anglers can do well with double-dropper setups cast to or from the bank. Let the rig sink on minimal slack and slowly tighten the line. Hop your insect 6 or 8 inches; repeat throughout the retrieve. You can do the same with bobber setups. The key is to never move the bait faster than it would naturally.

Moving-Water Presentations

Most bank fishermen prefer streams or rivers to lakes. This is because the spots where fish hold and collect meals with little effort are easy to find and fish—except in the really large rivers. Currents help in presenting insects that have little natural movement of their own, such as larvae. Moving water keeps fish facing upstream while it masks your movements and approach noises.

Upstream Vs. Downstream

Limited by their tackle, early fishermen started fishing downstream with live insects and, later, flies. Even then fishermen used long rods and very light horsehair lines to fish upstream whenever upstream winds made it possible. Because fish face upstream, casting upstream allows the angler to make contact with a fish before it notices him.

Most methods, however complex, relate to this rather simple strategy. If you see the fish first, you should be able to catch it most of the time. Today, new gear makes upstream insect fishing relatively easy if you understand how fish "see." Even though a predator fish's vision overlaps to provide binocular vision, which gives depth perception for capturing fast-moving prey, a 30-degree blind spot over the tail is present. If you stay within the blind spot and use the correct presentation, you will catch fish. This sometimes works better in theory than in practice, especially in overgrown streams or in water that is too swift or deep for wading safely.

A bobber rig will make upstream fishing easier than a weighted bottom rig. It extends the drift and lets you observe your bait better even if there is a lot of slack line. With a long rod, you can also control drifts by mending the line. Shorter casts that are required with light, delicate insect baits help even more because there is less slack and more accuracy. Dapping avoids the problem entirely.

Dapping: Dancing Or Skipping Insect Baits

If you dance an insect on the surface without the leader touching the water, you can forget about tippet size, surface drag and hook weight. Dapping, the British term for this deadly method, works well with any floating or adult insect. It's the best bet on windy days because the line will bounce the bait on the surface naturally for you.

However, insect-dapping works best if there's a hatch and rise. If there's no rise, then literally "beat the bushes" for terrestrials such as grasshoppers that can be fished on top or opt for larvae or critters like catalpa worms that might naturally flip out of shoreline vegetation onto the water, causing fish to feed. Don't worry about missing out on the first rises—fish seem to bite better at the end of this kind of hatch than at the beginning! Dapping also works in still-water situations under overhanging trees and in areas where adult insects dance on the surface to lay eggs.

Downstream Hoppers

Like other terrestrials, hoppers never move upstream. Two different presentation systems maximize results with floating hoppers. The first method, which usually works best, represents an injured or waterlogged hopper that's easy to catch. Either rig the unweighted hopper on ultra-light gear or float a hopper hooked to a 2-foot leader under a casting bubble for greater casting range. Cast this rig upstream at an angle of 20 percent or greater to a spot where the natural drift will run the hopper past lurking fish.

Fast reeling is required to keep the line reasonably taut, and it's important to keep the rodtip pointed at the hopper. As the hopper passes your position, either back-reel or let out slack; then quickly reel in and cast again. If there is no surface action, switch to a float rig and use split shot to sink the hopper.

Best used as a backup for windy conditions, the second rig imitates the action of a hopper that just blew into the stream. It works nicely where a meadow lines the bank if you fish from the downwind side. (If you must fish from the upwind side of the stream, you should dap instead. It's also a bit easier to dap after dark or when you can't quite control slack line in a free drift.)

Cast the hopper about three-quarters upstream, as close to the bank as possible. When fish are shy or the water is very shallow, cast onto the bank and gently pull the bait into the water without any excessive slap or line cast. Let the bait float several feet. Then begin a rapid retrieve of the hopper to simulate an insect trying to scoot off the water. Hits will be easy to detect; a tight grip on the rod is recommended in case the hit is by a big brown or a smallmouth.

Topwater Action After Dark

On the most heavily fished lakes and streams, the crowd of anglers, water skiers and pleasure boaters usually clears out at dusk when the fish start to bite best. Nothing will do more to improve your results on heavily fished waters than fishing at night, where legal, or fishing the first two hours after dawn and the last two hours before dark. Wherever you can, consider fishing all night; the action usually peaks during the full moon. Use water temperatures as indicators of when to fish—early morning or evening.

Insects fished on top seem ideal for nocturnal action because their silhouettes will stand out against the lighter night sky. Grasshoppers, crickets and big moths all produce.

The key to good nighttime results seems to be intensive effort expended within a limited area. Even though it's possible to troll at night along lighted docks or roadbeds, it's almost always more

Some of the day's best action may occur after dark. Anglers often will work around boat docks and piers for gamefish that move into the shallows, looking for an easy meal.

productive to concentrate on a single structure, pool or riffle.

Lighted bobbers allow you to watch your bait's drift while offering a small clue about casting distance. However, it's best to arrive at the selected spot when it's still light and practice getting your casting distance just right. Because weeds, stickups and other hazards are less obvious at night, you should double your normal line test and use heavier tackle. Fish can't see your line after dark, anyway.

Mid-Depth Drifts

In very small streams, a drifted cricket might start out as a topwater bait, sink to mid-depth and finish on the bottom. Even here a bobber can help. A "mini-land-mine"-shaped Thill float rigged so one shot is above the bobber works even better than an

Insect, Larvae Presentations

unweighted bait because the upstream shot ticks moss and rocks, creating a slower, more natural drift. In shallow water where up-stream casts don't always work, this allows a longer cast and drift so you can reach downstream fish.

On larger waters, the normal unweighted or lightly weighted bottom presentation works with both insects and larvae. On streams that are more than a cast wide, you should work the off-side away from paths. In such cases, a bobber rig may work best to slow yet control your presentation.

The basic medium-river system for insects does not differ, ex-cept for hook sizes, from that used with worms or leeches. Bulk shotting with bobbers for quick depth changes works in water of uneven depth. More delicately graduated shot presentations work over more even bottom.

Reversals And Backwaters

If you let an aquatic insect go around and around in a spinning eddy or through a reversal (an eddy with a horizontal axis), you can take fish. When the spinning current is too broad to cover with your rodtip, opt for a bobber. At times, nothing else works as well as a bobber with a graduated shot string and a bait to match bottom.

Over rocks, try stone flies or hellgrammites; over mud, go with a caddis or water worm. Stick to bottom-bouncing methods dur-ing the day. Move to mid-depth approaches before or after the sun hits the water and try topwater baits after dark. Only the most cautious approaches will work because fish may be "pointed" in just about any direction for all-around aerial defense.

Moving Bait, Pine-Cone Drifts

At times, it's impossible to move a bait directly downcurrent from a boat or the bank. A sliding sinker rig can do this in many cases. Cast it to where the current starts and let the weight sink. Open the bail and the bait may slide downstream as line runs through the sinker. If the bait does not move because of a deep band of slack water off bottom, try a Biggie rig. Just adjust the bob-ber size to provide the proper amount of flotation needed to move your bait downstream.

Another way to get your bug into downcurrent action is to hook onto a floating stick or pine cone that takes your line downstream. Then simply pull the line free and fish out the cast. This works well with cased caddises in slow-moving meadow streams, too. For faster moving streams, the stet-pegging system mentioned in Chapter 4 works great.

Bottom Plonking

Fishing a bait in one spot with a dropper or fish-finder rig is a popular method for the beginner. It's not a bad presentation over reasonably hard bottom with dragonfly nymphs or other substantial baits that can be seen for some distance. However, it's a dead loss if your bait simply burrows down out of sight of passing fish.

Still-water methods work in holes with not more than 4-mile-per-hour currents. Just remember to keep the weight and bulk of your terminal tackle as light as your rod and line combination will handle.

Special
Bait Situations

18

Preserved And Other Deceased Baits

D ead and preserved baits, with the exception of salmon eggs and various odoriferous catfish baits, rarely work as well as live baits. This is because they lack movement and freshness. Then, too, live baits must be fresh; this isn't always the case with frozen or improperly preserved baits. Where conditions are tough, such as in the declining salmon fisheries on the West Coast, those who enjoy experimenting move from the traditional anchovy cut bait to live anchovies with presentations such as mooching.

Obviously, rigs that present preserved baits in the most natural manner work best. Salmon-egg hooks with turned-up eyes and increased hook gaps work well with eggs and roe rolled along a streambed. Trolling harnesses shape and better present dead minnows in today's tough fishing conditions.

Because they can't provide the movement that increases their sphere of discovery, preserved baits usually require rigging systems that produce and accentuate movement. Frozen worms can be rolled downcurrent or, like preserved minnows, strung on an in-line spinner and cast or trolled. Dead grasshoppers can be dapped effectively under cutbanks where trout lurk. Crickets slowly worked on a floating jig head can tempt bass or panfish. Movement masks the preserved nature of the bait. This movement can be provided by the retrieve, current or, in some cases, a live bait on another hook or lure.

The main advantage of dead bait is convenience. Easily kept

216   Complete Angler's Library

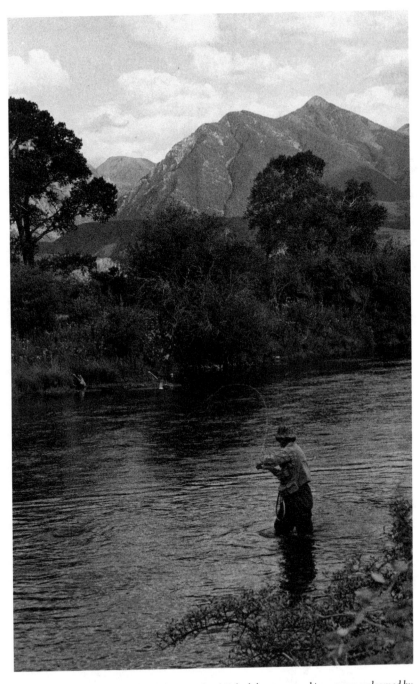

Even fly fishermen who usually rely on "artificials" find that preserved insects are welcomed by trout. If presented properly, dead insects can be an effective bait.

Preserved And Other Deceased Baits   217

bait allows savvy anglers to tote baits so they can continue to switch until something works.

Drawbacks to dead bait are equally obvious. Not all preserved baits are properly prepared or stored. Repeatedly frozen and thawed bait stiffens and smells, making it unacceptable to most gamefish.

Frozen Fish Baits

"Recently deceased" baits usually work best. If the frozen bait container smells too much like fish, it's probably been thawed and refrozen. Whether the bait is fresh or not can be determined by the look of its eye, its smell and feel. If the eye is blood-shot or sunken or the bait smells fishy or feels soft, leave it for catfishing addicts.

Bring only what you need for bait. If you carry more dead minnows than you can use, the seagulls and terns just get a feast. Pound and 2-pound blocks of fish or squid hold too much bait for a day. These can be slowly thawed at home and the outer layers of bait can be removed while those inside are still frozen. Rewrap or repack baits into smaller containers; you will save money and enjoy a better bait selection.

All dead bait should be frozen as quickly as possible. One way would be to layer minnows or other bait onto a cookie sheet covered with a piece of newspaper; then set the cookie sheet on a freezer shelf. If the baits are not touching each other, they freeze fast and can be stored in a plastic bag for use anytime within a couple of months. For longer storage, coat the bait with ice to prevent freezer burn and improve bait quality. This involves dunking the frozen baits one or two at a time in a pot of ice cold water and removing them quickly. Once the thin ice layer forms on the baits, return them to the freezer. If you think a thicker coating is needed, repeat the process. This will radically improve bait quality and length of storage time.

Freezing enough bait to last a season is easy with baits like shad, smelt or eels that offer "seasonal surpluses." These come to net or trap in such numbers during their "runs" that freezing all of them makes sense. Freezing recently deceased bait that was purchased live and iced down when it turned belly-up also adds to your season's supply.

Baitfish size should match that of the prevalent baitfish

Larger bait shops often carry packaged frozen bait. It's convenient, especially if you have some freezer space devoted to storing bait.

schools. It saves sorting time at the water to freeze fish by size. Another reason for freezing is to maintain the proper-sized bait throughout the season. Later in the year, smaller baits like those that work best for crappies may not be available as minnows grow larger. Such small baits also may be just the ticket to tempt logy lunkers during the summer doldrums!

Freezing Other Baits

Freezing baits in water ensures top quality because it eliminates oxidation and freezer burn for storage periods of up to a year. Small bits of bait can be bagged with just enough water to cover in a sealed, plastic sandwich bag. With the top of the bag open, stand it up in a tray in the freezer until frozen; then seal the bag. When you get more of the same kind of bait, put it in the bag,

Preserved And Other Deceased Baits

pour in more water, reseal it and repeat the freezing process.

You can also freeze worms, wigglers, scuds or grasshoppers in ice cube trays full of water. After these are frozen, pop the baits out of the trays and store them in plastic bags in the freezer. Even when you are using live baits, a handful of frozen bait cubes dumped in a small Styrofoam container containing several refreezable cooling packs can offer a useful alternative when your prime bait does not produce.

It's also useful to divvy up an assortment of minnows, clams and crayfish tails so you have two or three of each bait type in a bag in your ice chest. This is a great emergency kit when the usual baits aren't working.

For longer trips, you may want to pack frozen baits on a mix of ice and rock salt—5 pounds of rock salt in a 40-quart ice chest—instead of just ice alone. This creates a colder-than-usual slush which keeps frozen baits fresh for a longer time period. It's also a good way to carry your catch home.

Ice fishermen who face the reverse problem can pack their ready supply of frozen bait in black plastic bags. On sunny days, this speeds thawing. Baits frozen in ice cube trays, like wigglers, can be put in a sealed, plastic sandwich bag and thawed in a pocket. (Be sure the bag is tightly sealed if you want to stay dry.)

Catfish addicts might consider frozen or rejected fish, clams, squid and mussels sometimes available in fish markets.

Freeze-Dried Baits

As backpackers know, freeze-dried food doesn't taste like the real thing—even though the shrimp come close. Freeze-dried items are frozen at fairly high vacuum so the liquid boils off. Then, these items will keep as long as they stay dry. As tackle-box or boat-locker stash, freeze-dried baits are a great emergency item. They keep until you add water. Freeze-dried baits include frogs and other amphibians, shiners, minnows, grass shrimp, crayfish, grasshoppers and more. No other method works so well for special baits like frogs. Baits in sealed, plastic sandwich bags can even be removed one at a time as needed.

Freeze-dried baits need to be soaked in water for only 20 minutes or so before use. Warm water speeds this process a bit; however, hot water should not be used because it cooks and softens the outside of the bait before the inside is thawed. (If they are used before they are fully reconstituted, fish will still bite, and the freeze-dried bait will be a little more tender.)

Standard-dried, as opposed to freeze-dried, baits include minnows, crickets and grasshoppers. They are soaked in a preservative first, then dried. If dried "as-is," these baits will start to mold if they get a little damp because the regular drying is not as complete. Some claim these preservatives "put fish off." If this is a concern, spray the bait with a fish-oil-based lubricant or attrac' tant to mask the preservative's smell.

Salt On The Tail

Salting removes the liquid from baits, toughening and preserving them. Salted herring used as a sturgeon or catfish bait works great. Oily fish, like herring, seem to reconstitute the best.

Salting your own bait isn't difficult. Mix non-iodized salt and sugar. Some use half and half, some use 25 percent sugar, 75 percent salt. Spread about a half inch of the mix in a plastic or stainless steel container. (Don't use aluminum or iron!) Carefully space the fish so they don't touch. Layer in more salt, then more fish until the container is full.

Baitfish not more than ½ inch thick should be ready in two days at 55 to 75 degrees. Thicker baitfish might take an extra day. After this, pour off the brine and refrigerate the baitfish for up to three months. A vacuum-seal bag system increases the shelf life of small amounts of salted or dried bait.

Salted, air-dried minnows work nicely for catfish. Dried grasshoppers take trout and float nicely, providing some interesting surface action.

Preserved In Alcohol

Minnows and baits such as grass shrimp also can be preserved in formaldehyde or isopropyl alcohol. This is an acceptable substitute where fresh, frozen or freeze-dried baits aren't available.

It's easy to put up your freshly caught baitfish in jars or square plastic containers with sealing lids found in most kitchens. Stick in as many baitfish as possible, reversing heads and tails to increase capacity. Add isopropyl alcohol to within 1 to 4 inches of the container's top. Tap the container carefully so any bubbles float to the top. (Bubbles hold air which may oxidize and spoil your baits.) Add two or three drops of anise oil or fish scent to

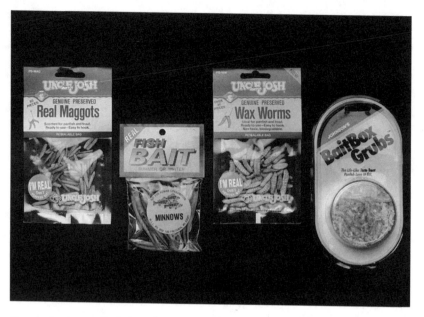

If you're having trouble finding or keeping live critters for future fishing excursions, then the preserved baits may be just the thing for you. They're easy to store and to carry with you.

cover the alcohol smell. Keep the container in a cool, dry place. In areas where goldfish aren't legal as bait, some anglers will add orange food coloring to the preservative to color their minnows.

Radiation Works, Too

Radiation treatments are used to sterilize baits packed in plastic bags and other containers so they can be stored for long periods at room temperature without spoiling. This method kills the bacteria that cause the baits to spoil and decompose. Because the radiation is not long-lasting, there is no danger. This system eliminates the need for pretreatment preservatives and produces an even more natural result than freezing.

Salmon Eggs And Clusters

The question of whether eggs fresh from the salmon should be considered "live bait" or not won't be answered here. Clearly, salmon eggs—alive or dead—are the prime bait for trout, steelhead and the other species that feed on fish eggs.

It's equally clear that the best salmon eggs are fresh. With fresh eggs from a ripe hen you need only dust on a bit of salt or borax, wrap the eggs in waxed paper and keep the roe skeins or separated eggs cool in the refrigerator until you're ready to use them. If you need to keep eggs for longer periods, you need to spend more time and effort in order to properly preserve these precious baits.

All salmon-egg curing processes start with separating the skeins or carefully cutting them in chunks. (Some use hot water to separate eggs from the membrane; others use screening. Both methods work with moderately hot water and moderately abrasive rubbing.) Then hold your salmon eggs in cold water—non-chlorinated spring water works best.

Spawn chunks are best cut up with an exceptionally sharp pair of scissors into inch-square pieces. Include a bit of the tough skein membrane with each chunk. This helps keep the eggs together.

Preparing Egg Clusters

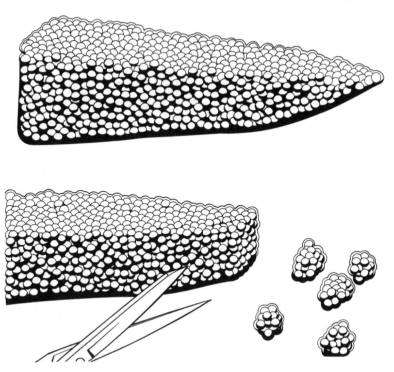

As this illustration indicates, salmon eggs are best processed in spawn chunks which can then be cut into approximately 1-inch-square pieces, the right size for use as bait.

Preserved And Other Deceased Baits

Chunks can be wrapped in regular cheesecloth or special red, fine-textured mesh used for commercial spawn bags. Cut off the excess material after each square is tied.

In most home salmon-egg cures, borax is used to coat the egg chunks or preserve the eggs after they have been removed from the skein. About two pounds of dry, non-detergent borax are needed to preserve two skeins from a salmon. (Don't use the detergent type unless you want your fish to foam at the mouth!)

The method is as simple as drying the egg skeins or cutting clusters and rolling them until well-coated. Store them in an inch-deep layer of borax in an airtight container for about two weeks. The borax washes off when the eggs hit the water. (If you want to store them for a longer time period, you will need to freeze the containers and contents.)

To process individual eggs, take well-rinsed eggs that have dried for about two hours and plump up the eggs in a solution of one teaspoon boric-acid crystals to one quart water. Once the eggs firm up so they feel like peas, they're ready for the container—usually a small jar. Small, sealed, plastic sandwich bags also work.

Sodium sulfate—available at photo shops and chemical supply houses—preserves egg clusters and skeins at least one week longer than borax. Mix sodium sulfate with equal amounts of non-iodized salt and brown sugar. (A cup of each will be sufficient for eggs from a couple of big salmon.) Put half of the mixture onto a cookie sheet covered with newspaper which absorbs excess liquid. Place the drained and dried eggs or clusters in a single layer. Sprinkle on the rest of the mixture and stir. Let set for three hours or until eggs pucker up.

At this point, eggs can be stored in sealed containers in the refrigerator. The night before you go fishing, stick the eggs in a small container and cover them with water; add some salad or fish oil if you like. Eggs will plump up from the oil.

A simple sugar-and-salt cure works, too. After the eggs are separated, make a solution of one part sugar to four to nine parts salt in a glass or stainless steel container. Add only enough liquid to cover the eggs. The solution should run at least 80 percent on a salinometer. (Check stores that sell meat-packing items for one of these handy gadgets.) You could also add enough salt to "float an egg." And, pour in a teaspoon or two—see package directions—of aniline dyes for that zippy red, scarlet or golden color.

Tennis-Ball Bait Holder

An old tennis ball makes a good bait container. Slit its surface and put some worm bedding inside along with your bait. When you need bait, just apply pressure to both sides of the ball to open your container!

Gently stir the mixture for about 20 minutes. Drain the eggs, pack in an airtight container and refrigerate. You can also add oil to the packed eggs. If you fish where it's warmer than 50 degrees, a solution of 5 percent formalin or 1 percent sodium benzoate can be added to the curing brine. A teaspoon of anise oil per gallon of brine improves the result, too. (This system, with increased time for soaking, also works for egg skeins cut into chunks and usually fished with a netting or thread wrap.)

A slit tennis ball holds a day's supply of eggs away from sun and air. A 2-inch-long slit works nicely. When you squeeze the ball, the bait's available. This system also can carry a few worms in commercial worm bedding, as well as other similar baits.

All egg and cluster rigs present the problem of keeping eggs or clusters on the hook. Fortunately, a number of devices work. Spe-

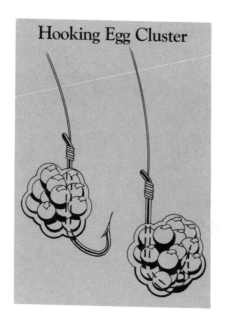

Hooking Egg Cluster

An egg cluster can be a fairly durable bait if part of the membrane remains intact. Slip the cluster on the hook as you would an egg, turning it into the hook's gap as shown.

cial salmon-egg hooks carefully sized to barely fit inside eggs are necessary for use with single eggs. The up-turned eye increases the effective gap and improves hooking percentages. Because home-packed eggs may not be uniform in size, you might, for example, use a loop-to-loop system which enables you to quickly switch between No. 12, 14 or even 16 hooks.

Leader-loop rigs, as well as wraps with self-adhesive and regular thread, help hold on clusters. Clusters can also be covered with fine mesh and fished on single or treble hooks. Some anglers add a bit of yarn to the hook or tie it immediately above the hook's eye. You can saturate this yarn with the oil from oil-egg packs so you know you have fished out every drift—even if the eggs fall off the hook.

In still water, salmon eggs should only be fished on sand or gravel bottoms, and there are no problems with scavengers like sculpin or crayfish. The traditional "Shasta sandwich" combination does a good job here, as do other systems, such as the Biggie Bobber, that move the egg off the bottom increasing its sphere of discovery.

Single eggs, egg clusters and spawn bags can be fished off of most worm and insect setups, too. In still water, sliding sinker rigs, as well as windbeater bobber rigs which were discussed in

226   Complete Angler's Library

Chapter 4, produce. In calm weather, eggs work nicely when drifted just off the bottom of streams and rivers with the usual graduated shot-string bobber setup. Over-shotting a bobber rig so you can immediately hook a fish when the bobber comes up out of the water can produce on days when nothing seems to work. This is a particularly good method for big-water brown trout!

Egging In Moving Water

In moving water, bait placement—especially during salmon's and other species' spawning runs—seems more critical than bait type because fish such as salmon and steelhead often won't move far from their holding water. Baits are cast just at the upper edge of the redds, or fish nests, and fished with a moderately slack line or off a bobber where the bottom is reasonably even. The bait should drop just fast enough to hit bottom just below the redd where steelhead lurk. After a line mend, you can continue the drift downcurrent for about 30 feet. Move in tight below prime spots. The reduced casting distance should offer added accuracy.

19

Combining Lures, Baits

Consequently, if all the experts who develop and sell sprays for lures and various stink baits are right, and tests seem to show they are, hanging appropriate live bait on lures should improve the lure's smell and taste without ruining the lure's action. Just don't, as one beginner tried to do when told of a "sardine-wrapped" lure solution to the lock-jawed riverine salmon, wrap on a whole sardine that is twice the size of the lure.

Most experts agree that a match of lure and bait color works best in clear water. A silver spoon or spinner runs nicely in front of a rainbow smelt, for example. In murky water, lures with the more visible "hot" colors seem to work best. For topwater combinations, only the bottom color counts. In most cases, this is either white or black. At night, anything goes—black is the most popular choice.

Lure Size And Speed

Smaller lures and baits fished on lighter outfits for usually smaller fish has been the most popular approach. It works best where fishing pressure has increased or conditions, like those in clear water, are tough. Exceptions to the "smaller, lighter" rule include the massive suckers freelined for big bass in the South or dragged behind serving spoon-sized spinners for pike, muskies, striped and largemouth bass. Seven- or 8-inch-long sirens hooked to floating jigs for largemouth bass call for large jigs, too. How-

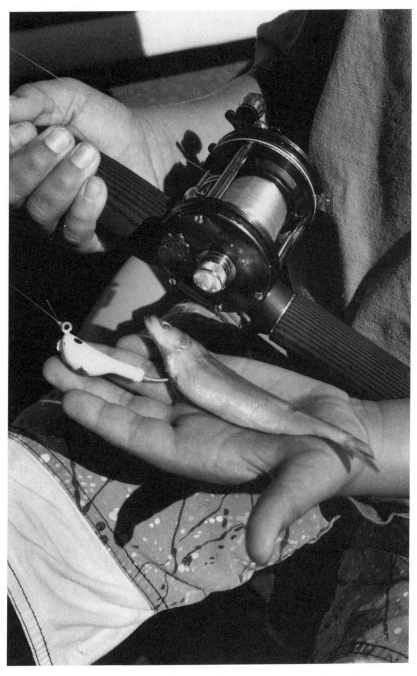

A shad on a floating jig is a potent combination for lake trout in the Great Lakes. This is just one of many combinations of lures and baits that have proven to be highly effective.

Combining Lures, Baits

ever, if an angler chooses a lure a size or two smaller than usual, results will improve when the lure is combined with live bait.

These lures should be retrieved more slowly, too. With bait-fish, the rule seems to be about 1 mph per inch in length. Insects and other baits are slower. Some, like crayfish, make a quick but short dash, and then stop. If in doubt, dump a natural bait into a water container or shallow water and note the speed at which it moves. Then poke the bait with a stick and see what it does to escape. Imitate that action in making the retrieve.

One advantage offered by plug lures is depth control, and except for ice lures, lateral coverage is an important plus when you aren't sure where fish lurk. Aside from slab spoons and ice-fishing jigs, plug lures are less successful at vertical coverage.

Once you have established the productive depth for the day, it's not difficult to choose a lure/bait combination to fit the situation. Lures, especially plugs, run shallower than the manufacturers claim because anglers generally use heavier lines and more hardware than the manufacturers do in their tests. With a bait added, plugs will run even shallower because the resistance increases on the troll or retrieve. If you determine the "real" trolling depths over bottoms of known depth, you will improve results. While you are doing this, you also should test lures for their optimum action by either trolling them alongside the boat or retrieving them at various speeds in a situation where you can see how they behave. Most lures have a range of peak performance that will vary once a bait is added.

Without some kind of tempo control, anglers will reel at different tempos. Some long-play types crank at 33 rpm; others are wired to reel at 78 rpm. This difference in tempo is one reason why lure favorites vary in performance. Two fishermen can retrieve at the same tempo with different reels and attain different speeds. You can do this because reels may vary in retrieve ratio or spool diameter.

Lures fished too slow, too fast, too deep or too shallow decrease your chances for success. If you take the time to think about the probable location and speed of the bait you're using, you can double your chances of success without adding any fancy gear.

Plugs

The biggest problem with a plug-and-bait combination is too

Strips cut from fillets are used as "sweeteners" for both spoons and jigs. Note that a strip is attached in several places to make sure it stays with the lure. A stinger hook has been added to jig to counteract "short bites."

much bait. For example, the classic sardine-wrapped banana plug, such as a Kwikfish, remains popular with backtrollers searching for salmon that, more often than not, forgo their feeding habits when they return to their natal streams. The key to effective plug action plus bait attraction is attaching a small 2- or 3-inch portion of a baitfish fillet between the two hooks on the lure.

A Flatfish, the other popular banana lure, often is adorned with short bits of nightcrawler or whole redworms draped over some of the lure's treble hooks. A little bit of bait "sweetener" goes a long way, and the plug action should be checked after you add bait (to make sure it's not radically changed). This is especially critical for trolling; the unbalancing that can result from the added bait can cause lures to spin. Deeper running plugs with larger bills and "fat plugs" seem less likely to become unbalanced than long minnow plugs; they are recommended for the addition of bait. Using fat plugs also lets you keep the total length more natural—an important factor to many gamefish.

If you hook minnows or other baitfish onto the plug, hook the bait on the in-line or trailing treble to reduce the chance of spin. Worms and leeches seem to affect plug action least if hooked in pairs on the outside points of the front treble. Cut-bait sweeteners can be wrapped between the trebles like a "sardine-wrap."

Minnow-shaped plugs are more difficult to bait because their action is more delicate. Generally, bait sweeteners work best on the lure's trailing treble hook. This placement seems to change the balance the least; however, it speeds up the plug's wiggle. Pectoral-hook placement of sweeteners is often best with the slower wobbling plugs, like the banana shapes.

On some minnow plugs, you can remove the rear treble, replace it with a single hook and lip-hook a minnow. However, a more effective system involves the use of a trailer hook with a 12- to 15-inch-long snell off the rear hook. A worm, grub or other tidbit is added to the trailer to tempt short strikers.

For a totally authentic presentation (at least to the angler's eye) run the worm dropper off the line 2 feet above the plug so the plug chases the other bait.

J-plugs, in which the line passes through the plug to a trailing single or treble hook, work with trailer minnows because the hook doesn't affect the action. At the end of the line that runs through the plug, attach a snap swivel and hook. If you like, add a 12-inch trailer leader with a No. 6 hook. Vary the trailer bait; sturdy but small lip-hooked chubs work. At temperatures above 50 degrees, try leeches; below 50 degrees consider worms. In brackish water try the combination of a shrimp chunk and a live marine worm. Experiment! Some really strange-looking combinations, such as mini-marshmallows and cheese, will take fish. Today's lunch may be tomorrow's trout treat!

Floating jigs, as well as topwater poppers in frog finish, help present small frogs in lily pads or around standing cover. Single-hook panfish hoppers used with lip-hooked, small minnows are effective in heavy summer cover. The minnow should be hooked barb-up to improve the action.

Spoons

As a rule for casting, longer, heavier-bodied spoons handle bait add-ons best. The Johnson Silver Minnow, in particular, is both well-balanced and virtually weedless. It works well with both worms and lip-hooked minnows. Check the spoon's action without bait against its action with bait. If the action changes too much, you probably need either a bigger spoon or a smaller bait.

Basic Steelhead Rig

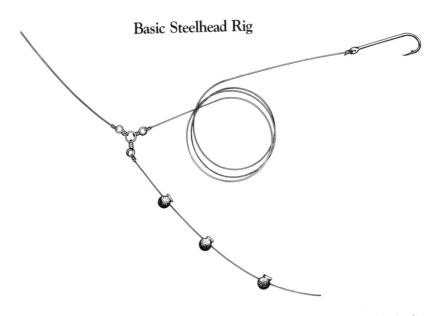

Known as the basic steelhead rig, it represents the basic three-way swivel rig for fishing live bait on a dropper hook. In this case, split shot is attached to another dropper in case of snags.

The alternative is a trailer hook tipped with worms, grubs or a minnow or a main-line dropper for your baited hook.

Main-line droppers particularly work well with slab spoons, the heavy-bodied, mostly plated spoons used to go deep fast. To effectively jig over suspended fish, such as striped bass or walleyes, adjust the dropper length to influence the bait's action. Make sure the dropper is attached to the line a foot higher than its length from the lure. This keeps the bait from getting snagged on the lure. The rule is simple: The longer the dropper, the less the dropper bait moves vertically during each jigging motion. With a 6-inch dropper, there is a faster, jerky motion. With a 6-foot dropper, a more gentle movement is the result. Choice depends upon your bait type, quarry species and the day's conditions.

If the dropper knot-to-lure distance is half as long as the dropper's length, your chances of a snagged dropper are reduced when you cast. For trolling light spoons, consider using a small spreader to reduce the chance of dropper baits putting kinks in your line. This seems less of a problem with heavy spoons.

Trollers also use flashers and dodgers—oversized spoons designed to attract—in front of live baitfish, whole dead baits and

Combining Lures, Baits

plug-cut herring. The larger the flasher or dodger in relation to the bait and the greater the angle between its parts, the more effect the flasher or dodger will have upon the bait's action.

Spinners and Spinnerbaits

Single-hook, in-line spinners, particularly the weight-forward types that reduce line twist, work exceptionally well tipped with worms and minnows. However, like spinners with off-line eyes and spinnerbaits, they do not eliminate line twist. It's important to pay close attention to lure spin either by watching the trolled lure from the boat or checking lures at the rodtip after the retrieve to make sure the rapid spinning doesn't result in line twist. Spinner blades can be modified to spin left or right by nipping the blade. With duplicate spinners and a ball-bearing snap swivel, you can reverse the spin by changing lures and baits every few casts. Trollers can keep line reasonably twist-free by using a trolling sinker like a Bait Walker that won't spin, a keel-type sinker or a trolling keel with or without swivels.

When conditions are tough, freeline spinners rigged directly to the line without a body just above a minnow, leech or worm can make a difference. Natural bait action is enhanced because of the spinner's light weight and flexibility. However, a bead should be used to protect the hook knot. Two small spinners rotating in opposite directions, such as in the case of smaller trolling rigs commonly used with worms or minnows, can improve results. At worst, they reduce line twist.

Commercial rigs, such as Ford Fenders, are popular; however, it's easy to make your own using a knot or wire line crimp as a stop above the terminal spinner, clevis and bead. Small Colorado-blade spinners provide just enough weight for casting hellgrammites and other aquatic larvae. Elongated baits, such as red worms or leeches, require a larger hook to keep the worm from spinning. Shorter baits, such as crickets, require two single hooks rigged "ice-tongs" style to reduce spinning. For deeper presentations, use narrower spinner blades that spin and sink faster. (This works great when you are fishing nightcrawlers for walleyes or sirens for black bass.)

Spinners without bodies sink the slowest; hollow beads and glass beads sink faster. If you add a metal body or, for really fast sinking, a lead head and leave the bail open, you will reach the

Complete Angler's Library

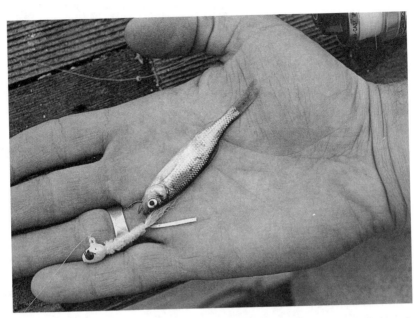

A minnow is used as a "sweetener" on this jig. The minnow is purposely lip-hooked upside down. It will try to right itself, creating more erratic action and movement in the water.

desired depth quickly. At the other end of the sink rate spectrum are wooden-bodied spinners that float at rest.

Spinnerbaits work the same way. If, however, you add a jig for casting weight, the chance of a fish hitting the lure as it helicopters attractively to the bottom on slack line improves. Worms, leeches and salamanders are ideal partners for spinnerbaits offering the additional advantage over in-lines of less line twist and fewer hang-ups. (If you make your own spinner and spinnerbait rigs, leave a ³⁄₁₆-inch stub on the aft eye wire that you use to secure the worm or minnow. You can also thread your bait's head over the hook eye and pin it in place with wire or a toothpick.)

Jigs

Jigs—whether floating or the usual sinking types—offer the casting weight needed to best present a minnow, worm, leech or amphibian. Tiny ¹⁄₃₂-ounce and ¹⁄₁₆-ounce jigs on No. 8 or 10 hooks are the ice angler's choice for larvae and insects, as well as tiny minnows for use under bobbers for crappie fishing. They also work when fishing other baits in awkward situations that could sacrifice expensive lures.

Combining Lures, Baits

At times, it's useful to offer baits like worms in a jig format with nonstandard hooks. To make your own, simply clamp a large split shot just behind the eye of a hook with a 6X (six times the regular length) shank. By threading on an appropriate-sized worm, you eliminate short hits and keep the bait from balling up in the bend.

Dressed jigs with skirts made from hair, plastic and other materials are well-suited to delicate baits that tend to be lost during the cast. Even if your bait sails away over the blue, you still have something that fish will strike at the end of your line.

Weedless jigs are good for presenting amphibians in heavy cover. Stand-up jigs with slanted heads improve the presentation of worms or leeches. Best of all, jigs tied directly to the line are often less expensive than rigs that include hooks, sinkers and swivels. Double jigs, two minicrappie jigs baited with worms or minnows, double your chances of success and carry casting weight small enough to interest panfish and trout. Sometimes, double jigs drop a bit faster than, for example, catalpa worms. In this case, replace the upper jig with a floating jig for a more natural drop. This system works well with worms over snags and cover.

Flies

Flies can replace jigs in the previously mentioned rigs if the baits offer sufficient casting weight. For example, freelined minnows can easily haul around flies tied to dropper loops off the main line. Ice flies, wet flies, nymphs and streamers all benefit from an appropriate sweetener like a larva or a piece of worm that's proportionate to the hook size. The hook's shank length is a good measurement.

Other classic fly-and-bait combinations include a live mayfly and a dry Cahill or a caddis fly and an Elk Hair Caddis. Both offer trout and panfish the sight, smell and taste of a live insect. As a bonus, you can continue to fish out retrieves with the fly even if the bait is lost during the cast.

Rigs with large streamer flies, like the two- and three-hook Demons and Terrors common in New Zealand, can be tied with a streamer on the front hook (or hooks) with a minnow trailer added. Such rigs with a leech or worm trailer also troll nicely.

If short hits are a problem, which is often the case on hot, summer days, reduce the size of the fly and trailer bait or add a short

Complete Angler's Library

"kicker" leader loop with a tiny No. 10 or 12 treble at the trailing edge of your bait. With minnows, the tip of the tail's top lobe is a good location. Where regulations limit the number of hooks, you may need to troll a single-hook, standard streamer or use a single-hook kicker. As a rule, single-hook kickers are a size or two larger than trebles. You can tie these rigs at home with loops for the fly like the commercial loop-to-loop systems which save you time on the water.

Ultra-Light Combinations

On extremely slow days or in clear water, use ultra-light gear. Even though you may only have temporary custody of some fish, bait hooks and minilures don't cost much. Any action is, for the most part, better than a day without strikes.

Attach a casting bobber 3 to 4 feet above a tiny spinner-fly or spoon-fly sweetened with a small worm chunk or small minnow. This easy-to-cast system is a killer for river smallmouths, most trout and other lockjawed species that won't take big lures.

It's the ideal beginner's outfit because it can't sink deep enough to snag if a cast is muffed. It is great for children and anyone else who enjoys cast-and-retrieve action rather than sedentary still fishing. It's also a fine rig for areas where weeds grow to within a couple of feet of the surface. By adjusting the bubble to lure length, you can vary the running depth to suit conditions.

Combining Lures, Baits

20

Baits For Ice Fishing

Without a doubt, the more unproductive the fishing is for average ice anglers, the more advantageous it is for live-bait specialists who have the action and smell of various baits in their fishing arsenals. In the slow-motion world beneath the ice where fish survive in below-normal dormancy temperatures, it's not unusual for fish to go days—even weeks—without feeding. As metabolism slows and appetite fades, fish are slow to respond to any stimulus—even the tastiest of live-bait entrees. Treats like little bits and pieces of maggots, waxworms, wigglers or other larvae may be nudged or nibbled unenthusiastically if you don't use too heavy a line. Visibility is so good under the ice that even 4-pound-test line may look like anchor rope to these lackadaisical eaters. Panfish specialists, for example, have moved to much lighter lines—even down to a fraction-of-a-pound-test rigs.

In the clear water under the ice, fish will see a moving bait from greater distances than a stationary bait; however, they may hit a bait only after it has stopped moving. Expert ice anglers often alternate slow jigging with motionless presentations to attract the fish. A minute or two after the jigging stops and the line and bait are motionless, these fish may gently inhale your bait. (You can't really call such minimal movement "a bite.") It's not uncommon for anglers to use a jig to lure fish within range of a lighter outfit tipped with a tiny hook and a silver wiggler or mousie.

Larger fish will go for these tiny baits and, at times, minnows

This nice catch of panfish and perch emphasizes that ice fishing can be both fun and productive. A key to success in taking panfish is using extremely light test line and live bait.

that are often fished under tip-ups. Dual-bait systems—a minnow for movement and attraction and a maggot or other tiny bait rigged on a dropper to treat finicky appetites—also work.

Cold water and colder air can turn monofilament lines into something between a mini-Slinky and an unusable mess. Some lines become weaker in cold weather; others fall victim to abrasion from the constant scraping against the edge of the ice. Special "cold weather" line, which remains more flexible in freezing temperatures, deserves a try. Consider line color, too. Uneven lighting conditions on the ice can make the clear lines you need under the ice disappear. Some anglers use blue line, others mark the line in some way at hole level.

Ice fishing baits generally are so small that they won't sink very fast on their own. Ice flies and spoons, as well as tiny shot and lead wire, are used in this situation. Whenever possible try two drop-pers or a lure-and-bait combo and a dropper. (Of course, no mat-ter where you fish, be sure to familiarize yourself with the fishing regulations for that locale.)

Even where you jig lures, tie on a 14- or 15-inch-long dropper 2 feet above the lure. Add a No. 16 hook and a single Eurolarvae or maggot and, more often than not, the fish will strike the drop-per. The extra length reduces or, depending upon the bait and dropper's test and flexibility, eliminates bait movement which might discourage shy fish. It also keeps the dropper hook from snagging on the bottom.

Years ago, most ice anglers tied droppers above their ice fly or spoon. Today's anglers prefer to tie the dropper to the lure's hook. This probably works best right off sand, gravel and other firm bot-tom. Drop your lure to the bottom, pull it up a foot or so and jig, then stop. The bait settles back onto the bottom where fish may be rooting up bottom baits disturbed by the jig. Instead of a bare hook, consider using a sparsely dressed dropper fly tipped with a maggot or Eurolarvae. Maggots do drop off hooks. (That's why some fishermen use three or four at a time.)

For fish on a biting blitz in deep water that aren't picky about rigs, consider using a heavy dipsey sinker and two or more dropper hooks to shorten sink time. Some ice anglers rig this on a heavy pike outfit so they can haul in as many fish as possible until the blitz ends. Heavy dipsey sinkers can also carry up bottom sam-ples—which is useful when you're looking for a particular species over a mussel bed, for example. Smear some beeswax into the hole containing the sinker's swivel stem. Drop the sinker, work it up and down a few times and pull it up. Bottom samples should be attached.

Better Bobbers

Bobbers remain the easiest method to detect bites when bait fishing under the ice. Using the smallest possible float lets you in-stigate action when fish are being picky eaters. With a bobber giv-ing you a better idea of what's happening, it's easier to set the hook at the right time. Spring bobbers or jigging methods don't always do this because sometimes you merely pull the bait out of the fish's mouth.

But bobbers often will "hang up" in the chunks of ice and slush in a hole. Spring tips wired over a standard rodtip maximize sensitivity. Not all are springs, however; the technology stems from the British swing-tip system that's popular with match fishermen on streams and still water. With the ice anglers' spring tip, line is run through the spring bobber eye, then down through the standard rodtip guide. A narrowing of the gap between the two tips will indicate the very lightest bites. The spring tip can also be rigged as an extension on the end of your rod.

For panfish and smaller trout or lockjawed fish, it's difficult to use gear that is too light. Try 2-pound-test line, a No. 16 hook baited with a maggot and the smallest float you can find. Some, like the Thill Mini-Shy Bites are so small that they suspend $\frac{1}{128}$th of an ounce only! In fact, these floats are so light that you must find some minuscule "mouse dropping" British shot, or you need to balance the bobber with wire. (Wrap a little lead fly-tie wire around a toothpick, remove the toothpick, thread your line through the opening and pinch it tight. Add or remove wire until the bobber barely floats.

Fixed ultra-minifloats work well down to about 6 feet of depth. Below that, however, you need a slider bobber and a bit more weight. (You don't want to waste too much time waiting for baits to drop into the productive zone!) Stay with the same elongated, light floats mentioned previously. Such floats work well with red worms and, in the larger center slider sizes, with the extremely small minnows that are usually used for crappies and other panfish.

Sliders work best when rigged with a stop knot or a commercial bobber stop. Stop knots also are good depth indicators for jigging and spring-bobber fishing. With sliders, two baits often work better than one when conditions are tough. Worm-and-borer and maggot-and-minnow combinations work. Center sliders, in particular, work reasonably well unless you're dealing with zero and sub-zero temperatures; then, spray them with a lubricant to reduce line freeze.

Sliders work with minnows hooked through the lip or dorsal fin. As minnow size increases, use less weight to float the bobber higher in the water or use a bigger bobber (if sensitivity is not that important). When nibblers are merely mouthing minnows, nip a piece of the bait's tail to decrease its action, producing that "easy meal" look that winter fish appreciate.

Minnow Methods

Tip-ups improve your chances of success with larger fish like walleyes, northern pike or muskies that cruise under the ice. Because the tendency is to concentrate on your own jigging or bait hole and forget about tip-ups until a flag goes up, using rather large, hearty minnows as bait makes sense. Four- to 5-inch-long chubs, as well as large shiners which are durable in cold water, work. Changing minnows every time you check your lines keeps bait lively.

Minnows keep nicely at typical winter water temperatures. Just cut a hole in the ice and submerge your container of minnows. If you cover it with a piece of home-insulation board, it won't freeze into the ice quite as fast.

Minnows can also be used as sweeteners for larger ice jigs and big ice flies. Where two or more rods are allowed, you can also fish two rigs. A smaller-than-usual, extremely sharp No. 6 or 8 hook can be hooked under the dorsal fin of a minnow or baitfish; add a tiny split shot and fish this through a second hole. Using a smaller-than-usual hook ensures that fish have plenty of time to take the bait if your attention is diverted. Start this presentation just 12 inches off the bottom. If there is no action, raise the bait another 2 feet off the bottom; then, pull it up to within 3 feet of the ice. Yo-yo the bait 3 to 5 feet up and down until you find the productive depth. This usually will be about where the plankton and zooplankton concentrate small baitfish. This level seems to rise during the day and drop back toward the bottom at night. If you find fish hitting minnows in fairly deep water, switch to a rig with a terminal dipsey sinker and a dropper hook placed at the productive depth. This radically reduces the time it takes your minnow to reach the hot depth.

Your primary rig—the one you either jig or watch most closely—is best set up with either a bobber-and-bait outfit or a double dropper, offering panfish a choice of spikes, wigglers or Eurolarvae in varied colors, that doesn't have to be constantly jigged. Take special care to brace the rodtip, keeping it steady, so you can spot those light nibbles like a pro.

Hook several baits on each hook. That way, any lost baits will help concentrate fish. Where chumming is permitted, a slow, sparse dribble of mashed egg shells or ground bait or spikes helps. Big gobs of chum satiate fish instead of tempting them.

A small lure sweetened with a mousie and jigged off the bottom was too good for these fish to pass up. But, be prepared for light bites that usually are barely noticeable.

Jigs, Baits And Trailers

Sweetened jigs and spoons, minnow-type lures such as Vertical Rapalas, tiny live minnows and latch strips add extra attractant when conditions are tough. Many experienced ice anglers always use sweeteners. In fact, some never use unadorned hooks because if a bait is lost, they still will have some attractant in place.

Ice flies, jigs and spoons come in just enough colors and sizes to ensure you've never got the right model with you. If in doubt, opt for smaller sizes, duller colors and, as conditions worsen, less rod movement. A dropper with a maggot can help. At times, brightly colored Eurolarvae work; more often than not fish bite best on the usual boring brown, cream and tan baits. Changing lures and baits eats up time on the ice. Consider rigging with leader connectors that offer quick hook, sinker and lure changes.

This will allow you to move from minnows to wigglers to grubs to salmon eggs and back fast. Some anglers pre-tie rigs for particular situations and baits. Wrap these on corrugated cardboard holders marked with the appropriate information and use loop-to-loop ties to speedily change from rig to rig.

Bites On The Drop

Bites that occur before your bait reaches its working depth are a major problem with all types of baits, as well as with popular lures like the Swedish Pimple. Gamefish will hit some baits on the drop because they appear injured or dead. The problem is that an angler not expecting this may not react until it is too late. How many times are baits nibbled off your hook before you know it? With antenna or even center sliders, it's possible to see the tilt that indicates the bait has moved off to the side—even on the first drop in a new hole! Also, if you count down the time it takes for a bait to sink during the first drop in any new hole, you will know when a fish has taken your bait on later drops. The habit of centering your rodtip and the bait over a hole is a good one to establish. If your line either stops moving or starts creeping to one side of the hole, you probably have a fish. (Clean holes with smooth edges make it easier to see what's happening in the hole. A slotted spoon or one of the nifty scoops used to remove cooked items from a wok can free up a hole in one swoop.)

Snooping With Sonar

No matter how carefully you have chosen your bait for ice fishing, you won't be successful if there are no fish in the area. That's why portable sonar units are almost standard equipment for ice anglers. All you need is a sonar unit with a transducer, rechargeable storage battery and some sort of carrying case. You can cobble up a good rig in an insulated case like a Styrofoam ice chest capable of holding a standard 6-volt or 12-volt battery and a spare— larger-capacity motorcycle batteries are a good choice—and, of course, the fish-finder unit. Because cold batteries rapidly lose their juice, some savvy anglers will include a hand warmer in the battery box to maintain battery life.

Flashers which can still be found at flea markets and such work well for ice action. Manufacturers produce portable liquid crystal units; however, many anglers simply take their units out of their boats to use. Because the transducer's face must be in liquid to function properly, set it in vegetable oil or windshield washer fluid on the ice, level it and begin prospecting for fish locations. Some anglers use small home levels for leveling the transducer; others glue a photographer's level to the transducer. (Anti-freeze is not a good choice for the liquid contact under transducers. It's a pollutant and illegal in many areas.)

Thoughts On Sites

"So much ice, so few fish" is the challenge faced by those who ice fish. Finding the fish remains the biggest challenge. (The best live-bait techniques won't work if fish aren't in your bait's sphere of discovery.)

As a general rule, fish can be found in winter where you found them in summer and fall. Points, natural springs, inlet streams, drop-offs and structure will attract fish. However, because the water is fairly uniform in temperature, fish will cruise more than might be expected. Do not stay in one place too long if the fish are not biting.

Safety First And Last

Safety should always be the No. 1 concern for ice anglers. Inflatable flotation life vests should be worn at all times. They provide emergency safety buoyancy in the water, as well as insulation under your parka on the ice. You should exercise extreme caution when driving a vehicle onto the ice, including following established trails and driving with the vehicle's doors open. Learn from experts. Stay with a group, if possible, and, to maximize safety, always carry a throwing line. When in doubt, don't go on the ice!

Index